REDWOOD WRITING PROJECT

INQUIRY AT THE WINDOW

INQUIRY AT THE WINDOW
Pursuing the Wonders of Learners

PHYLLIS WHITIN AND DAVID J. WHITIN

HEINEMANN
Portsmouth, NH

Heinemann
A division of Reed Elsevier Inc.
361 Hanover Street
Portsmouth, NH 03801-3912
Offices and agents throughout the world

The authors and publisher wish to thank those who have generously given permission to reprint borrowed material:

Portions of Chapter 1 first appeared in "Inquiry at the Window: The Year of the Birds" in *Language Arts* (vol. 73, no. 2, February 1996). Copyright 1996 by the National Council of Teachers of English. Reprinted with permission.

Fig. 4-1 from "Variation in Black-capped Chickadee Group Size" by André A. Dhondt and James D. Lowe. From *Birdscope* (vol. 9, no. 1, 1995). Reprinted by permission of Cornell Laboratory of Ornithology.

Library of Congress Cataloging-in-Publication Data

Whitin, Phyllis.
    Inquiry at the window : pursuing the wonders of learners / Phyllis Whitin, David J. Whitin.
        p. cm.
   Includes bibliographical references (p.).
   ISBN 0-435-07131-9
    1. Science—Study and teaching (Elementary)—United States—Case studies.   2. Inquiry (Theory of knowledge)—Case studies.
3. Questioning—Case studies.   I. Whitin, Phyllis, 1948–   .
II. Title.
LB1585.3.W55   1996
372.3'5'044—dc20   96-34233
                                     CIP

Editor: *Leigh Peake*
Production: *J. B. Tranchemontagne*
Manufacturing: *Louise Richardson*
Cover design: *Darci Mehall*
Cover art by *Ashley Layne*, student

Printed in the United States of America on acid-free paper
99 98 97 EB 1 2 3 4 5 6 7 8 9

CONTENTS

ACKNOWLEDGMENTS

From the beginning both parents and teachers nurtured us as inquirers. Phyllis traces the interest she has in the stars and birds to the long hours of observation with her parents. David appreciates the support that his mother gave him observing the majesty and mystery of butterflies. Our parents were our first teachers and we extend a special thank-you to them for helping us look closely at the world. We are indebted to some wonderful teachers at the University of New Hampshire who helped us grow as teachers: John Chaltas taught us the power of asking open-ended questions and fostering a sense of inquisitiveness in all that we encountered; Mike Andrew showed us the importance of messing about in science and the benefits of building a scientific community in our classrooms; Jon Emerson taught us how to draw out the natural curiosity of learners.

A heartfelt acknowledgment goes to Carolyn Burke of Indiana University with whom we shared our rough-draft thinking as we wrote this book. Carolyn is the quintessential collaborator who helped us appreciate the details of our story but also pushed us to examine the conditions that made that story possible. We appreciate the helpfulness of teacher Pat Pearman, who assisted us in detailing the benefits of a long-term study. We thank naturalist Rudy Mancke, who shared his professional perspective with us and helped us connect the work of our children to the work of the larger scientific community. His enduring curiosity of the world was a powerful demonstration of inquiry itself. We thank Jim Kelly, owner of Wild Birds Unlimited, who graciously donated so many materials. He also shared his genuine love of learning by encouraging children to be naturalists in their own right.

We thank Leigh Peake at Heinemann, our brilliant guide, who helped us envision the big picture and still pay attention to the small details. She was always there when we needed her, and her sense of humor made this project a most rewarding and enjoyable one. We appreciate the work of Joanne Tranchemontagne as well, who gave such careful attention to the many details in the production of this book.

And lastly, we extend the warmest thank-you to the children in portable classroom #1, who taught us what it really means to inquire about the world. They were the ones who led the way and gave us a year like no other. Their questions about what they saw out the window extended our own curiosity and helped us grow not only as reflective practitioners, but also as more sensitive wonderers about the natural world. For this nurturing and growth we are eternally grateful.

INTRODUCTION

Natural history is something that everyone is curious about. I think curiosity is innate, but in a lot of people it's latent; it's right under the skin . . . They're not really aware of it until they're put in a situation, or unless they have a parent or a teacher who is willing to develop the latent curiosity for them.

—Rudy Mancke, Naturalist

This book is about latent curiosity, and how it came alive for a classroom of twenty-six fourth graders. It is a story that began simply by looking out the window, observing and wondering about nature with the support of a community of learners. And it is a story that left us with a changed vision of learning.

Throughout the book the reader will hear several voices. By fortunate circumstances, this adventure was led by two adults. Phyllis is the regular classroom teacher. David teaches at University of South Carolina and works collaboratively in this classroom. During the fall he was present in the class one or two times a week, but during the spring he was on sabbatical leave. We are quick to admit that many of the events in this book would not have taken place in this way without those conditions. However, we are grateful for the opportunity to investigate the processes of inquiry so closely, and we are committed to find ways to create parallel conditions in different classroom situations. We have merely gained perspective on inquiry, and we invite readers to continue the conversation.

Rudy Mancke's voice permeates this book. He is a former high school science teacher who currently hosts an educational television program. He leads teachers in developing naturalistic studies in their classrooms by offering workshops in schools. We had the opportunity to meet with Rudy on several occasions, and he advised us about important ideas to highlight with the children. He believes strongly that first-hand experience must be the beginning point for scientific study in schools. He was fascinated with snakes as a child and became a voracious reader in order to pursue his questions about these reptiles. He relates that in college, however, his view of teaching and learning was revolutionized by a geology professor, John Harrington. Harrington insisted that the key to education was reasoning. He constantly challenged his students to construct the story behind geological facts, thereby drawing conclusions and forming generalizations. Throughout this book we quote Harrington's book, *To See a World* (1973, 1994). His words have influenced us as they have influenced Rudy Mancke. Harrington relates a fascinating story of the world's history while preserving a sense of wonder and awe about its mystery. It is this sense of wonder that unites Mancke, Harrington, the children, and us.

As we reflected on the year's events in preparation for this book, we struggled to find a way to express our current understandings about the inquiry process. We decided to create a visual analogy to capture our thinking. We found that creating a visual about inquiry became an act of inquiry itself. For this reason we feel it is important to share its evolution with the reader. As we searched for a meaningful analogy, we wrestled with the tension of highlighting a part of the process without losing the whole.

A vacation at the ocean gave us our first opportunity to reflect on the holistic nature of our story. The awe and mystery of the ocean conveyed for us the power of inquiry itself. People feel small next to its power and enormity, yet they long to explore it, to know it, and to savor its beauty. The ocean holds a comforting rhythm with its predictable patterns of tides, paralleling the inquiry cycle of observing, questioning, theorizing, and more observing. Although both the water and the sands constantly shift, they are always connected to the whole. Similarly, in inquiry, the focus of our explorations shifts from time to time, but a sense of wonder connects the whole process. With the sea edge in mind, we sketched a rough, irregular shape to outline our metaphorical model. We also decided to symbolize the flow between key ideas by omitting defining lines between them. We placed wonder in the center, where it would touch and sustain inquiry itself. We arranged the key ideas that had emerged from our reflections around this center. Next we shared our sketch with colleagues, whose perspectives helped shape it into its final form. This metaphor became the framework for our thinking and our writing.

When Carolyn Burke compared our sketch to a flower, she helped us extend our metaphor in new ways. We wondered which species of flower might best symbolize our metaphor, and we decided upon a petunia. In many petunias, the richest color is in the center, and this deeper color bleeds outward onto the petals. We found this idea fitting to convey the way wonder permeates inquiry. The arrangement of the petals also could symbolize other important ideas. The petals touch and overlap as well as blend with the center. So too exploratory conversations, a critical use of resources, careful observation, and other conditions overlap each other, while they all remain firmly connected to the center of wonder.

The interlocking parts of the petals also demonstrated to us that the separations which educators often create really obstruct our ability to understand the process of making sense of our world. Dichotomies such as fact and fiction, teacher and learner, and young child and professional blur and disappear when inquiry is rooted in wonder

Finally, it was important that the petunia shows life. Life connotes change, growth, and movement. We were reminded of the words of Vygotsky: ". . . it is

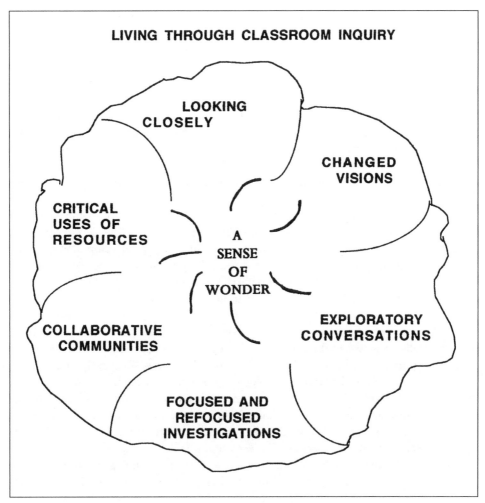

LIVING THROUGH CLASSROOM INQUIRY

LOOKING CLOSELY

CHANGED VISIONS

CRITICAL USES OF RESOURCES

A SENSE OF WONDER

COLLABORATIVE COMMUNITIES

EXPLORATORY CONVERSATIONS

FOCUSED AND REFOCUSED INVESTIGATIONS

FIG IN–1   *Living Through Classroom Inquiry*

only in movement that a body shows what it is" (1978, pp. 64–65). Inquiry moves. To study its nature we must study it in movement. The image of the petunia helps us convey the feeling of vitality that a community of inquirers experiences.

This metaphor for the essence of inquiry also influenced our organization of the book. First, we do not tell the story of this yearlong inquiry chronologically. A sequential story might convey a progression of thought, and we found inquiry to be an interwoven, spiraling process. We would also suggest a final resting place if we told the story chronologically, and we felt that connotation would be contrary to our intended meaning. Secondly, although we highlight the idea on one petal in each chapter, we do not proceed sequentially around the flower. Our intention is to demonstrate that all of these ideas work in concert. As one looks closely, one's vision is changed. Through collaboration, a learner is able to look more closely, and so forth.

However, Chapter One does begin at the beginning. We believe that inquiry is born by looking closely and marveling at the real world. The stories in this chapter stress that the importance of looking closely never diminishes. Over time inquirers learn to look closely in new ways. Conversing with members of a community supports further observing and raising new questions. Thus, looking closely is a beginning, but it is never-ending.

Chapter Two addresses a critical use of resources. We found that both adults and children discovered new and exciting resources throughout the study. We also discovered that the nature of our classroom conversations altered our view of written texts. The class developed a ritual of raising multiple questions about an observation at the window, and this stance led us all to question written and pictorial sources as well.

Chapter Three shifts the focus to the importance of exploratory conversations themselves in supporting inquiry. Children came to use the class as a public forum to raise questions, share current thinking, and to develop new perspectives. Through conversations children found opportunities to develop unique voices while contributing to the knowledge of the group.

Chapter Four shows that in an inquiry study, the attention of individuals or a group can be focused for a time on a particular aspect of a topic. Specific tools can support inquirers to take a unique perspective on their understanding. This chapter discusses two of these occasions of focusing attention on issues through the support of a mathematical perspective: studying the nesting cycle of a pair of bluebirds, and investigating an ecological problem of forest fragmentation.

Chapter Five addresses the importance of collaborative communities in supporting inquiry. At first we thought only of the class as community, but in time we realized that these learners were connected with multiple communities, such as families and members of wildlife societies. As we analyzed the learning in the class, and as these children communicated with adult ornithologists, we also came to believe that these children, although young and less experienced, were scientists in their own right. The more we read about the nature of scientific inquiry, the more we saw commonalities between young and old. For this reason we have paired stories from the history of science with the stories of these children.

We believe that the story of this study of birds is merely a window to the story of scientific inquiry itself. This realization is part of our changed vision of learning, and it leads us to Chapter Six, where we reflect on the nature of these changed visions. Again, with changed visions, the story never ends. For this reason, we have added an Epilogue as well. The "year of the birds" transformed our vision of inquiry, but it also raised new challenges. We wanted to take what we had learned about the essence of inquiry into a new school year. The Epilogue begins that story. So, in a sense, we end with a beginning, and we believe it is fitting to do so. For us, the window led us to view birds, but there are many windows through which we come to marvel at the world. We invite the reader to explore with us the many ways for appreciating and understanding the wonders, mysteries, and splendors of the world, and the wonder of learning itself.

1

Inquiry Begins with Looking Closely

Our year of inquiry began by accident. Shortly before school opened, Phyllis was in the attic looking for a box of children's books when she tripped over a discarded bird feeder. She immediately thought of her newly assigned portable classroom, with a crab apple tree growing outside one of the windows. An image of a child sitting by this window, watching and recording the daily activity of birds, flashed through her head. The feeder seemed to provide the perfect opportunity for children to engage in some scientific writing, and she shared her idea with David. We both believed in the importance of observation, writing for real purposes, and firsthand scientific investigations, so we decided to hang this feeder, along with a hummingbird feeder, in the little crab apple tree, and invite students to take turns observing during writing time and after morning announcements. We made a journal labeled, "Bird Observation Journal," hung it by the window, and waited for the birds and the twenty-six fourth graders to arrive. We thought that we might attract some sparrows or finches, but there was no way we could have imagined the adventure ahead that would change our visions of both the natural world, and of learning itself.

Learning to Look Closely

Birds did find the feeders. Rhiannon was the second person to make an entry* in the class journal, writing a detailed report about two hummingbirds:

> I saw two hummingbirds fighting over the hummingbird feeder. And they came back. I saw a bird nest in the tree. One came back and drank up and down seventeen times. They came back. The same two.

---

* All entries reflect edited spelling for the reader's convenience.

During our class meeting time later that morning, we invited Rhiannon to read her entry aloud. We told the class to be ready to tell Rhiannon what was particularly interesting about her description and to ask her questions. After she read, students told Rhiannon that they appreciated her careful observation of the bird nest and the seventeen sips. Next we asked if anyone had a question for Rhiannon that would help us understand her observation more clearly. We were especially careful during these first group meetings to give examples of helpful and hurtful questions for the observer. We reviewed with the children the difference between a question like, "Why didn't you tell how big they were?" and, "Did you notice about how big they were?" Rhiannon then called on volunteers for questions:

Scott: Did you see what color the birds were?
Rhiannon: They were blackish and reddish.
Shawn: How do you know it took seventeen sips?
Rhiannon: I counted.
Danielle: How do you know it was a sip?
Rhiannon: I saw the beak go into a hole.
Stephanie: How do you know it was the same two birds?
Rhiannon: They looked the same every time.
Eric: How do you know it got some of the water?

Developing Questions About Personal Observations

The first question about the color helped to extend her initial observation. Sometimes it is what children choose *not* to observe that leads to some interesting and productive conversations. Although Rhiannon did not record any information about color at first, her classmate's question caused her to expand her written description. In fact, later in the conversation Scott then extended this discussion about color even further by sharing his knowledge about how color is an important attribute to distinguish males from females. In this way the group opened another important dimension of the observations, and in the days that followed observers did record color carefully. The other queries that the children posed for Rhiannon questioned the validity of her observations, i.e., how did she verify it was a sip, or that it was seventeen sips, or that it was really the same two birds? The children posed these questions not in a belittling or condescending way, but in a truly inquisitive search for knowledge. Rhiannon could not really answer Eric's question definitively, and she simply explained that she assumed it sipped some water because its beak moved in and out of the hole. The children continued to raise these same kinds of questions throughout the year, helping them realize that sources of nonfiction, both their own and that of others, are open for examination, challenge, and debate.

Appreciating the Language of Scientists

Several days later Ashley wrote in the journal:

> I saw three or four hummingbirds . . . They took several sips. The humming-
> birds were yellow green color with a little gray, basically they chased. If one
> was at the humming feeder the other bird following would peck the other's
> body. One had a little reddish pink on the chest of the body. The food is
> going to be half gone because of one hummingbird.

Ashley's entry reflected the interest in color that had been raised by Rhiannon's
journal, and her classmate Jenny complimented Ashley on her precision. Ashley responded by noting that one of the hummingbirds was a female because it had no
red, extending her written text and drawing upon this male/female distinction
that the class was focusing on more and more. Stephanie complimented Ashley on
her use of the word *chase* to describe "how they were going around." Eric was intrigued by another word she used, and asked how she knew the birds were "really
pecking." Ashley looked a bit hesitant and admitted she wasn't sure if they were
"really pecking." David then asked the children, "What other words could we use
besides *peck*?" They suggested: *tap, bump, push, get the bird's attention, kiss* and *nudge.*
Each of these words conjured up different images; *peck* might convey fighting;
bump might suggest an inadvertent touch; *nudge* might imply a signal that birds use
to communicate while *kiss* could imply a breeding behavior. These early discussions about language highlighted for the children that in their role as scientists they
must be thoughtful about the kind of words they choose to use. They were learning that synonyms do not share identical meanings—that even among the words
they listed, they could make finer distinctions. They were also realizing that living
in a community of scientists comes with certain responsibilities—i.e., as they
shared their observations they must also be ready to support the language they use
to shape those observations. Regular writing and talking was teaching class members to take nothing for granted.

More discussions about language arose as the children continued to share their
daily observations. When Shunta described hummingbirds as "goldish" and "greenish" the children complimented her for the use of those words. Phyllis asked,
"How is the word *greenish* different from the word *green*?" The children said that
greenish implied "not a bright green," "maybe a little yellow," and "dullish." Here
again they were learning about the importance of scientists using precise, descrip-
tive language. The movement of birds also conjured up a variety of terms. When
Tony used the word *glide* to describe a hawk he saw flying above the classroom,
Phyllis asked the class, "What pictures in your mind does the word *glide* make you
have?" The children suggested: "wings out like a glider," "no flapping," "like sail-
ing," and "floating." By raising this question about "pictures in your mind" we

invited children to create multiple images for their meanings, and we believed that this fund of images would benefit their future writing, drawing, and observing. The class developed a chart entitled "Verbs to Show the Movement of Birds" that included *glide, sail, float, maneuver,* and others that the children generated throughout the year. We posted the chart by the observation window for easy reference.

Creating Metaphors to Describe Scientific Events

Kevin opened another avenue for description when he took his first turn at the window. Part of his report read, "It ate like a shark." He stopped reading at this sentence and demonstrated with his jaws a widemouthed hasty chomp with the accompanying sound effect, "grrrrrump." We invited the class to spend a few minutes talking about what images "eating like a shark" brought to mind. Chris said, "The bird grabbed the food." Kevin then refined his description by explaining that the bird was a messy eater and spilled a lot of food, emphasizing the speed of a shark's eating habits instead of its violent nature. In this way Kevin's sharing of his analogy helped him clarify and extend his initial observation. In fact, over the following months the class used the idea of "eating like a shark" or "eating like a pig" to describe the eating behavior of other birds and to compare eating habits at different feeders.

Kevin's spontaneous metaphorical language paved the way for using metaphor as a strategy to describe observations and concepts throughout the year. In December, for example, William reported that he saw three bluebirds by our newly erected nesting box. He said that two birds were in the box, and one was guarding. We asked him why he had said "guarding," and he explained that one had acted like a soldier guarding, flying back and forth. William read a great deal on the subject of military history, and we realized that he was interpreting territorial behavior from his own personal perspective. Shunta demonstrated this idea of personal metaphors further when she described a chickadee chirping, and the house finches joining in "sort of like a chorus." Shunta loved to sing and was a member of the school chorus.

On another occasion William brought the wing of a duck that his father had hunted to school, and he examined the specimen under a microscope. William noticed that the blood "looked like dirt particles." He wanted to know more about blood, so Phyllis referred him to a health textbook. After studying the text and diagrams, he wrote, "Our blood is kind of like a river in the body. My wonder of the circulation system is: Does the bird's body have a circulation system like ours?" William had followed a path of looking closely, describing his thoughts metaphorically, gathering information, and generating a new wonder.

The children's natural use of metaphor to convey their observations is a strategy that is clearly demonstrated in the larger scientific community as well. At age sixteen Einstein conducted one of his "thought experiments" to help him explain the nature of light and principles of relativity. He used a metaphor to describe his thinking, imagining himself riding through space on a "wave of light," looking behind him at the next wave (John-Steiner, 1985, p. 16). Another metaphor comes from the current research in DNA. Scientists have compared the action of DNA, the basic components of heredity, to a biological computer program that is some three billion bits long (DiChristina, 1995, p. 16). The use of metaphorical language is a natural link between the language of our children and the work of professional scientists.

As the children developed metaphors to describe what they were observing at the window, they grew to appreciate the metaphors of published authors as well. Throughout the year the class recited poetry chorally, and we kept favorite poems posted on the wall for everyone to enjoy. "The Eagle," by Alfred, Lord Tennyson, captures the power and speed of an eagle's plunge from a cliff, "and like a thunderbolt, it falls (Tennyson, 1989)." By sharing poetry together, the class learned the art of description and careful word choice. At the same time, they were enriching the aesthetic dimension of scientific observation. It is interesting that scientists in the field have acknowledged this marriage of science and poetry as well. John Harrington, a geologist, demonstrates the unique perspective of poetry when he describes "Song of the Chattahochee" by Sidney Lanier. Harrington says:

> Lanier paints a picture in changing rhythm and pace so that the reader can tell exactly where he is on the long profile [of the river.] . . . Hidden in those words is the recognition that the profile of the headwaters is full of falls and rapids with a stair-step descent. Two other verses picture the botanic beauty of Georgia hill country as hauntingly as the memory of any Georgia boy could duplicate. (Harrington, 1995, pp. 120–122)

Harrington, like Shunta, Ashley, William, and the rest of the class, demonstrates that looking closely involves observing, describing, and observing once again with an enriched sense of wonder.

Talking Together in a Wonder Journal

An appreciation for the role of wonder in observation led us to create another kind of class journal later in the year. The purpose of this "Wonder Journal" was for children to share their wonders, or unanswered questions, about observations they had made. We wanted to legitimize the right to entertain unanswerable questions and to support children in making these wonderings public for others to consider. Some of their wonders included:

1. I wonder why the chickadee went to the bluebird house and was looking in it. What do you notice?

2. I wonder why the juncos come and go.

3. I wonder, were the slate-colored juncos protecting their babies? But I did not see no babies. What do you think?

4. I wonder why birds land on the same side on a birdbath?

Probably the wonder that the children responded to most frequently was one that David wrote: "Rhiannon's mom noticed a chickadee cracking a seed (she came to visit after school). I noticed a towhee (at home) cracking a seed by turning it around in its beak and biting it. So my wonder is: How do birds crack open seeds? Tell me what you see. How many times does a chickadee pound a seed until it cracks open?" Over the course of six weeks several children responded to this wonder with observations of their own:

1. "I saw a finch on Scott's feeder. Well, I was very close to the finch; it got a seed and set the seed down and pecked at it to get the seed from the shell." (Ashley)

2. "I saw a bird that took a seed and crack [it] open with his claw." (Brent)

3. "I saw my bird pick up a seed and run its beak in the middle of the seed like a saw and the seed would crack open." (Danielle)

4. "I went to a pet store and a parrot was loose and it was eating striped sunflower seeds. And when he ate them he would crack them open with his beak, and then he would stick his tongue between the striped sunflower shells and get the seeds between the shell." (Rett)

5. "I saw a finch at the tube feeder. It took a safflower seed, I think, and it moved its beak left to right and the seed cracked open. The finch ate it." (Ashley)

By making observations public children can invite others into their private musings and give their classmates another focus for looking closely. It is interesting that Danielle and Rett shared observations that occurred outside of class (home and the pet store). When children share genuine wonders about real observations, they see the world differently.

Problems that Link the Children to the Scientific Community

Shunta highlighted an important dimension of living the life of a scientist when she took her first turn observing at the window. She was most eager for her turn to observe; in fact, she had been keeping her own personal bird journal since she could view the window from her desk throughout the day. When she recorded her observation in the class journal, she wrote a lengthy entry. However, when she read her description at sharing time, she said she was frustrated because it was hard to write everything down because "things happened so fast." We had not anticipated this issue, but we could identify with the problem ourselves as classroom researchers.

Encountering Problems While Looking Closely

When Shunta raised the issue, we realized that developing strategies to observe more closely is a legitimate problem that scientists face, and that addressing the problem collaboratively would be a valuable lesson. We praised Shunta for bringing her problem to the class; we pointed out that one of the benefits of working in a community is that it is a collaborative resource. We asked the students to suggest strategies to deal with the fast pace of observation, and we offered a few of our own. As a collaborative group we developed the following strategies:

1. Have two people watch the birds.

2. Have the observer talk into a tape recorder.

3. Use abbreviations when writing.

4. Draw a site map that observers can use to record bird position and movement.

5. Use a video camera so observers can revisit the activity later on.

Shortly thereafter the children implemented several of these suggestions: They developed some abbreviations to help them write faster, such as *hb* (hummingbird), *se* (seedeater), and notations such as ' and " to designate minutes and seconds. Frequently two or more children observed together during writing time. Volunteers sketched a variety of site maps, which we photocopied and kept in the bird journal to be used as needed. Later in the year we videotaped the activity in the yard, and the entire class could observe, compare ideas, and repeat significant observations in order to generate theories of bird behavior. This whole discussion was extremely important for the children: They were learning that they can only do what scientists do by confronting the problems that scientists encounter. Children will naturally face these problems when they have the opportunity to set their own investigations, observe closely, and pose their own questions. In turn, learners identify more closely with the scientific community when they solve problems collaboratively. Having learned this lesson from Shunta, we looked for other opportunities to highlight the problems of looking closely with the children.

About one week later Tony recorded in the class journal that he saw a hawk flying over the portable. One of the children asked, "How did you know it was a hawk?" and Tony replied, "I could tell by its flight." We then noted this experience of Tony's as another common problem of scientists, i.e., how to identify birds from afar. We solicited strategies from the children to address this new problem, and they suggested the flight pattern, the shape of the bird (silhouette), and its call. Eric mentioned that when he walks home he hears birds and animals in the woods. He even suggested placing a tape recorder on a stepladder beside the feeder so we could hear some of their unique sounds. This brief observation and conversation again highlighted the legitimate problems that real scientists encounter (Figure 1-1):

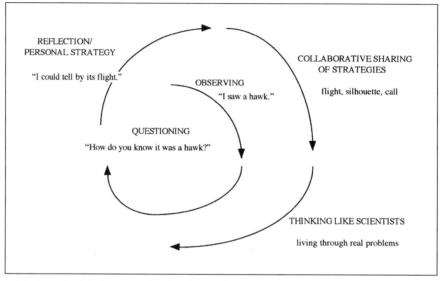

FIG 1–1   *A Model of Collaborative Problem Solving*

Tony's conversation about the hawk encouraged us to link the importance of questioning that we learned from Rhiannon's and others' journals with the issue of solving problems initiated by Shunta. Members of the community, then, helped each other by generating strategies and by developing language to describe experiences to an audience. These kinds of experiences encourage learners to reflect, and through reflection learners take charge of their own processes of learning.

The problem that Tony encountered of trying to identify a phenomenon from afar is a perennial problem within the larger scientific community. For instance, geologists must use indirect methods to understand the earth's inner structure. Seismologists learn from field and laboratory studies that the vibrations of earthquakes travel through different kinds of rock at different speeds. By looking for patterns and relationships in these vibrations they have constructed a picture of the earth's interior (Hornstein, 1993, p. 41). Other scientists confront this same problem of looking from a distance when studying galagos, little primates found in sub-Saharan Africa (Bearder, 1995, pp. 48–56). The problem in trying to learn about these creatures is that scientists rarely see them. These little bundles of fur, with flattened faces and long tails, hide during the day in tree hollows or well-camouflaged leafy nests, and only emerge at dusk to feed on fruit, insects, and tree gum. Since it is difficult to observe the details of the galagos' behavior, scientists have resorted to studying their sounds. Analyses of these sounds have provided information about their behavior patterns as well as the anatomy of the animals, for the sounds are influenced by the voice box and throat. It is this parallel connection between the experiences of the children and the work of scientists that continued to confirm for us the importance of having children confront real scientific problems.

Realizing the Limits of One's Vision

Finally, Brent demonstrated a third problem that served to link our class with the broader community of scientists. Early in September Brent noted in the journal that he saw a bird on top of the school. Several children commented that they had also noticed birds in various locations around the school grounds. Brent's comment encouraged the class to widen their vision and to notice activity away from the feeders. Understanding the limits of one's vision became even more important later in the year when the class was able to follow the entire nesting cycle of a family of bluebirds. The children were interested in where the adult birds found their nesting material, as well as food for the young. When the class was walking to recess, they spotted the bluebirds perched on a wire in the driveway and in an adjacent churchyard. Both experiences showed the class that part of looking closely is realizing the limits of one's vision. Scientists cannot experience the complex dimensions of natural events by viewing one locale in only one way; they must recognize that they know only part of the story. Brent's experience led the class to watch for birds farther from the classroom and to depend upon observations made by others in different contexts in order to more fully understand bird behavior.

Another dimension of the issue of limited observation is the importance of noting what is *not* seen. As the children learned more about the diversity of species of birds through field guides, they wondered why certain birds never came to the feeders. As a result they looked more closely at the unique features of our habitat and food sources. These observations were then compared with the features of other areas and with the needs of other species. During a class discussion in October, for example, Danny commented that he had noticed something interesting in his social studies book. The class was studying the Mountain West region in geography at the time, and Danny had noticed that the state birds of this region were much different from the state birds in the East. He explained that several western states had birds such as the mountain bluebird, while many states in the east selected the mockingbird or the cardinal. He reasoned that the west "seemed to be different" from the east.

Stephanie confirmed Danny's idea by sharing some information she had read. She had learned that a species of hummingbird only found in the west lived in a habitat of pine forests in mountainous areas. Stephanie realized that South Carolina does not have high mountains, and she used this example to show Danny and the rest of the class that the geography of a region influences where birds actually live. The observations by these children influenced later curricular decisions. We initiated more conversations that focused on the specific features of our region and contrasted them with those of other parts of the country. Our observations at the window were changing our understanding of geography and its influence on the ranges of birds and other wildlife. Months later, we had the opportunity to discuss these insights with Rudy Mancke, a noted naturalist. He also emphasized the importance of what is *not* seen:

> You are observing the birds that are coming to the feeder, but you should also be asking yourself, why aren't the others there? In other words, I see other birds out in the yard, but I never see those others at the feeder. Now what does that tell me? Even the absence of an animal from an area tells you something. Every time I think about this I think about my interest in Sherlock Holmes. If you take Conan Doyle's books, and you look, especially in the beginning, before the crime has occurred, and you're talking about Holmes and Watson and their views of the world, absence of something can also be a clue, can also tell you things. I remember one—the dog that didn't bark in the night. One of them mentioned the dog, and he said the dog didn't do anything, and the other one said, "Precisely." Because that tells you that the dog must have known the person who came in the yard because he *didn't* bark. There are birds at the feeder that come all the time, and then there are other birds that rarely show up. I saw a wren there once. It found a little larva in the seed. It wasn't interested in the seed, but it was interested in the larva. (Mancke, 1995)

Facing the problems of naturalists, developing strategies to address them, and digging for reasons to explain what was seen and not seen led us to identify some distinguishing features of inquiry. As teachers, we realized the value of struggling with confusing, complex, and sometimes frustrating experiences. Traditionally, schools have been organized to make things easy for learners, shielding them from the messiness, ambiguity, and challenge of intellectual ventures. This intent is the very antithesis of what inquiry learning is all about. Part of the role of the teacher is "*not* to step in front of the struggle" (Burke, 1995), but rather to highlight the problems that learners encounter and support them in devising appropriate strategies and possible solutions to the problem. When teachers grant children the responsibility to look closely, they also grant them the right to raise questions about what they see, the right to solve the problems they encounter, and the right to be empowered by the fruits of their struggles.

Using Tools Strategically to Look Closely

Tools support learners to look closely at their world and to express what they see. Tools such as the microscope or video camera helped the class examine details. Others, like rulers and crayons, enabled children to express their ideas. Tools came into play because learners wanted questions answered, wonders explored, and theories generated.

Models as Tools

One way that the children first used tools was to construct a model. The class had been observing hummingbirds, and the children were fascinated by the birds' speed, color, and size. One day Phyllis shared a comparison that she had read about: Six hummingbird eggs could fit in a teaspoon. To dramatize this point even further she brought a teaspoon to school and held it up so the children could visualize the relative size of the eggs. While she was talking Danny crumpled tiny bits of paper at his desk. He presented Phyllis with six balls of paper and she placed them in the teaspoon for all to see. The children were in awe that eggs could be that small. We had not thought of extending the model any further than the teaspoon, but Danny's crumpled paper eggs added understanding and wonder to the whole experience.

Technological Tools

Another tool for looking closely was a pair of binoculars. Early in the year Scott and Chris brought binoculars to school for the class to use; this new tool helped everyone look more closely at birds eating, preening, and walking on the ground. Similarly, the video camera helped us see—but with a new dimension. We taped the bird activity outside the window so that later everyone could watch together and interpret what was filmed. As they viewed the tape, we asked the children to write or sketch whatever they saw that was interesting; we also asked them to record a question as well as a theory for what they were observing. On one occasion the children were interested in the way the morning dove ate. Brent commented, "It looks like a chicken because when he walks he lifts his head up and down, he pokes the ground, and he keeps pecking the ground." Nikki said, "They eat really fast," and Eric described the behavior by saying, "It looks like they are hammering." The video allowed the children to look closely at a particular aspect of bird behavior that was intriguing to them and then describe it in multiple ways.

On another occasion they were interested in discussing color and the flock behavior of the birds in the yard. While watching cardinals, Shunta said, "This is a wonder I have: Why are all the females lighter than the males?" Deidre theorized that it is easier for females to camouflage with lighter colors and for males to show off to the female with their brighter colors. Ashley was also interested in the cardinals but for a different reason: "I wonder why the female and the male cardinals always come together. I mean, maybe it's protection for the female. I was just wondering about that . . . Because most finches, they come in just one big flock. And there's an odd number of males or females. And I wonder why so few towhees come at a time because there's a whole big flock of finches . . ." The video allowed learners the opportunity to revisit a particular behavior, such as the number of female and male finches, and look more closely at this inequality.

The videotape gave learners time to reflect on behaviors they may have been noticing and musing about for some time but never had a chance to share publicly. One such instance happened in March when we shared shots of cardinals and a tufted titmouse that we saw eating a peanut from our feeder. The eating behavior of birds had become a topic of interest all year and many children chose to focus on that behavior as they watched the tape. Here are some of their written observations:

Jonathan: Cardinals are messy eaters. Cardinals must like sunflower seeds.
Scott: I think the cardinal was eating a piece of egg shell. [The children had sprinkled egg shells on the ground because they had heard that eggshells are a source of calcium.] It was too big to be a seed.
Shawn: It's neat how the cardinal can find the same seed after dropping it in the seed pile.
William: Maybe the cardinal makes a pile of his favorite seeds [and] then eats them.
Rett: I wonder why the tufted titmouse will eat the peanut and the chickadee won't. I was wondering that because they're in the same family.
Danielle: I wonder how the tufted titmouse can keep that nut in his mouth.
Billy: A tufted titmouse was taking seeds and cracking them on a branch.

The children were interested in seed preferences as well as the style of eating; they wanted to know how birds held, ate, and selected seeds. This interest in eating was one they had been discussing throughout the year. These cumulative discussions certainly shaped what the children paid attention to as they watched the tape.

On another part of the tape some children looked closely at the color of bluebirds. Amanda drew some detailed drawings of the bluebirds perched on the wire as they were preening or holding a mouthful of straw. Lily wrote, "I saw a bluebird. It had lots of orange on it." Then in the left margin of her paper she wrote a letter to Phyllis: "Dear Dr. Whitin, Yesterday my Dad saw this bird. He didn't know what it was. But I saw the orange on it and said it was a bluebird. But he thought it looked like a house finch but then he saw the blue on it." This recent experience with her father was clearly in her mind as Lily watched the tape: Looking closely is influenced by previous discussions that learners have with other people.

Several children were intrigued by the nest building of the female bluebird and wrote about that:

William: I wonder how can birds make their nest round from straight straw.
Rhiannon: I think the longer the female bluebird stays away, the more she collects.
Amanda: I think she's getting bigger loads because she needs to lay her eggs.
Chris: A lot of times the female bluebird goes to the top of the building when she has straw. Why?

One of our goals was to have children not only observe closely but also wonder about what they saw and generate a theory to explain it. We felt that having a pool of theories to draw upon enabled learners to make further observations with a more enlightened eye. Throughout the year the class constructed theories about how birds ate, communicated, and "got along" with other species. As the children continued to make additional observations they carried these theories with them, looking to confirm, revise, or abandon them as new information became available. Most of the time we weren't really sure if our theories were accurately explaining what we saw. Rudy Mancke reiterated this point to us when he discussed the nature of scientific knowledge:

> I remember giving a talk to some high school science teachers one time and they were amazed that I was telling them it was O.K. to tell students that this mass of knowledge that we call science is very limited. We don't know all the answers. We shouldn't pretend to know all the answers. My argument to them was science is much better at observing and predicting than it is at explaining. In science we are often able to observe that something happens, and able to predict that it will happen, but we still don't know how it happened. For instance, we're not absolutely sure about tornadoes yet. We have some notion of cold air over warm air, and the movement of the earth, and so on, but we're not really sure yet. We're good at observing and we're getting better at predicting. (Mancke, 1995)

We wanted to instill in the children this same spirit of speculating about what they saw; we saw that encouraging multiple theories perpetuated this sense of wonder about what was transpiring outside the window. Observing, wondering, and offering explanations became the class ritual for looking closely.

Tools for Measuring and Drawing

Learners also use the tools of rulers and crayons, as well as the organizational formats of charts and graphs, to help them represent their observations. In the process of using tools to address their needs, they also learn how these tools operate in various contexts. One such instance occurred in March when the children began noticing the female bluebird building her nest. Children shared stories from home about birds building nests in their own yard. For instance, Tony said that he saw a cardinal building a nest "in a thicket behind my house" and Stephanie noticed a cardinal building one "about four and one half feet above the ground in a bush." Ashley brought to school a variety of broken egg shells that her grandmother had collected for many years. When David finally brought a copy of *Birds' Nests* (Harrison, 1975) to school everyone was eager to look at it because they had a real desire to know more. They wanted to know where certain nests were usually found, the composition and size of nests, who built the nest (only the female bluebird was building the nest, and the children were curious to compare this behavior to other birds), and the number, size, and color of the eggs. Since it was impossible to share this one book with twenty-five children, we made a chart for each child that contained much of the information that they wanted (Figure 1-2).

We tried to include species that the children were most familiar with, but some children consulted the book in order to find information on more unusual nests or clutch sizes. We invited the children to investigate some aspect of the data from the chart that seemed most interesting to them. Many of the children wanted to make models or life-size drawings. The chart contained a variety of units of measure: *mm* for the size of the eggs, *cm* for the dimensions of the nests, and *feet* for where the nest is located. We gave the children a brief introduction to these different scales of measure but figured they would become more accustomed to using them as they worked on their projects. Nikki, Rhiannon, and Danielle (Figure 1-3) made drawings of the eggs of certain birds. Nikki was intrigued by the differences in the eggs: "I used to think that all bird eggs were the same size." After actually drawing the eggs she even developed a rule of thumb for their general size: the length is usually in the twenties (mm) and the width is usually in the teens (mm). She hypothesized that the same size birds would have the same size eggs. All of these insights by Nikki were possible because she used a ruler as a tool to help her look closely at the size of these eggs. The active use of tools gives learners time to focus on a particular part of a larger study, providing the potential for new insights and additional theories.

Several of the children found some anomalous results as they measured their eggs. Chris carefully measured an assortment of eggs, cut them out, and laid them on his desk so that he could move them around and compare their relative sizes. He consulted the book on nests to get a wide range of egg sizes. After he made a model of the largest egg he could find—the mute swan's egg (112.8 x 73.5 mm)— he told Phyllis, "It's a really weird shape." He showed her his model, which looked like an elongated pea pod. She readily agreed, and they laughed together. Then they looked at the measurements, and Chris realized his error: "Oh, I only saw the 11 (instead of the 112 for the length). Since all the measurements on the chart were written as a two-digit number by a two-digit number, Chris did not recognize the uniqueness of this three-digit number. He laughed at his funny-looking egg and then imagined it standing on its end as he remarked, "If that was really an

	Size of Egg	Number and Color of Eggs	Size of Nest	Who Builds Nest	Where Nest is Found
Cardinal	25mm X 18mm	3-4,gray,green,wh,blue		F, some M help	Below 10 feet
E.Bluebird	21mmx16mm	4-5 pale blue		F, M rarely will help	Cavity in trees
Br. Thrasher	27mmx19mm	4, pale blue	12" o.d., 3 3/4l.d	F and M	Ground, bush, low tree 3-7'
House finch	19mmx14mm	4-5, pale bl/green,blk dots			Tree cavities, building ledges
Car. Chickadee	15mm x 12mm	6-8, white, red.brown dots	6 cm	M and F	5-6' above ground, hole in tree
W. B. Nuthatch	19mm x 14 mm	8 white,lt. br., laven.spots		M&F excavate, F lines	2nd cavity, 15-50' above ground
T. Titmouse	18mm x 14mm	5-6 cr. white/br. spots		uses holes they find	Tree cavity, 2-87'
Goldfinch	16mmx 12mm	5 pl. bluish white	7 cm. o.d., 2 cm l.d.	F	Fork in tree 1-33', average. 4-14'
D.eyed Junco	19mmx14mm	4-5 pl. bl. wh, br. spots		F, M sm. carries mater.	Ground,grass, tr. root, or tree to 8'
Hummingbird	13mm x 9 mm	2 pure white	3-4 cm. od, 2 cm ld	F	10-20 ft., slant-down branch
Towhee	23mmx17mm	3-5, cr. white, red, br spts		F	Ground, or 2-5' in bush, low tree
Blue Jay	28mm x 20mm	4-5 olive, tan, dk. br. spots	20 cm. od, 10cm, ld	F and M	10 - 25' in tree
Pine Warbler	18mm x 14 mm	4, gray-white, br. spots			30-50' horizontal limb pine, far out
Mourning Dove	28mm x 22 mm	2, white, unmarked			10-25', in tree, usually evergreen
Mockingbird	24mm x 18 mm	3-5, bl., gr, with br. spts	18 cm od	M and F	3-10' tree, shrub, vine
Starling	29 mm x 21 mm	4-5, pale bluish, unmarked	messy, 8 cm. l.d.		10-25 ', cavity, hole

FIG 1–2 Nesting Information

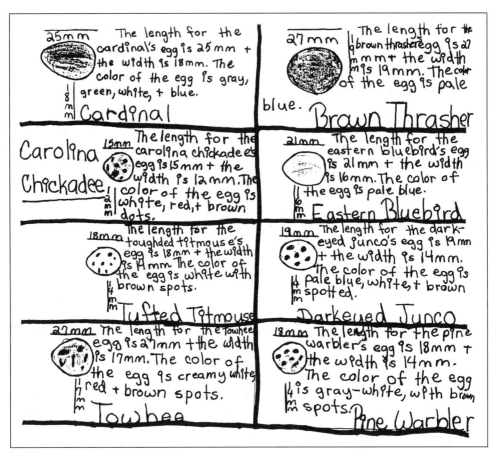

The length for the cardinal's egg is 25mm + the width is 18mm. The color of the egg is gray, green, white, + blue.
25mm
18mm
Cardinal

The length for the brown thrasher egg is 27 mm + the width is 19mm. The color of the egg is pale blue.
27mm
Brown Thrasher

The length for the carolina chickadee's egg is 15mm + the width is 12mm. The color of the egg is white, red, + brown dots.
15mm
12mm
Carolina Chickadee

The length for the eastern bluebird's egg is 21mm + the width is 16mm. The color of the egg is pale blue.
21mm
16mm
Eastern Bluebird

The length for the toughded titmouse's egg is 18mm + the width is 14mm. The color of the egg is white with brown spots.
18mm
14mm
Tufted Titmouse

The length for the dark-eyed junco's egg is 19mm + the width is 14mm. The color of the egg is pale blue, white, + brown spotted.
19mm
14mm
Dark-eyed Junco

The length for the Towhee egg is 27mm + the width is 17mm. The color of the egg is creamy white, red + brown spots.
27mm
17mm
Towhee

The length for the pine warbler's egg is 18mm + the width is 14mm. The color of the egg is gray-white, with brown spots.
18mm
14mm
Pine Warbler

FIG 1–3   *Danielle's Drawings of Eggs*

egg for a mute swan, it would waddle like a penguin!" Chris's knowledge of eggs helped him to question this glaring abnormality. The use of a tool in a meaningful context supported Chris as a sense-maker.

Jenny used inches instead of millimeters to draw some of the first eggs. She knew something was wrong when she looked at the unusually large eggs that she created. Jenny had read the measurement of the blue jay's egg, 28 mm, rounded it to 30 mm (3 cm), and then had used the scale of inches to make a line of three inches. She called Phyllis over, "Look, Dr. Whitin, this doesn't look right!" As with Chris, the context helped Jenny make sense of her work and revise her initial model.

Shawn had a different problem. He was trying to draw a round nest with a straight ruler and was having difficulty figuring out an appropriate strategy. He wanted to draw a nest that was 10 cm in diameter. We had explained to the children that the diameter was the distance across the nest but intentionally had not given any other instructions. We wanted the children to figure out for themselves how to construct a circle. Shawn started by drawing a square and seemed quite pleased that all the sides were equal (Figure 1-4). However, when David asked him if that shape was 10 cm across "in all directions," Shawn measured the diagonals of the square and found that they were much longer. He then drew just one corner of his square with sides that were 10 cm long, and then drew a line outwards from that corner between the sides that was also 10 cm long. He still wasn't satisfied because he saw that not all points along the edge of his shape were 10 cm across "the center." His use of the word *center* helped him. He and David talked about a diameter going through the center every time. Shawn next marked a dot on his paper, drew a series of 10 cm lines through the center (5 cm on each side), and connected the ends of those lines to create the nest he wanted. He then sketched several other nests and even helped some classmates who were struggling to make round nests themselves. In reflecting on what he had learned Shawn wrote, "I learned a new problem. It was how to make a round nest without making a mess-up . . . I learned that a bird's nest is all different sizes. Before doing this project I thought that birds' nests were all the same size." By using the tool of the ruler Shawn gained a new perspective about birds' nests in general and also a deeper understanding of what makes a circle unique.

Not only did children use the strategy of measuring to investigate the size of eggs and the size of nests, but they also looked at the size of the clutch. Billy used a graphic display to show the number of eggs found in each nest (Figure 1-5). He

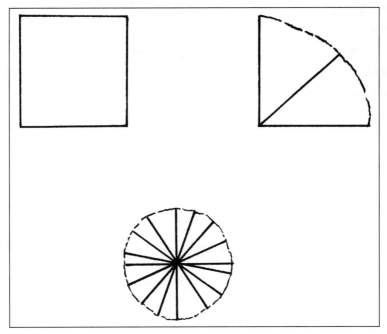

FIG 1–4   *Shawn's Attempts at Drawing a Nest*

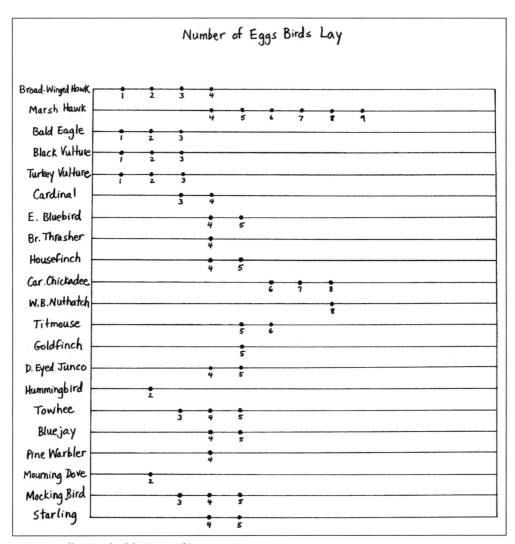

FIG 1–5 *Billy's Graph of the Range of Eggs*

then looked at the data in numerous ways. First he tallied the total for each number and found, "There were more 4's and 5's than any other number. I think [that happened] because it [4's and 5's] isn't a real small number or a real big number." Phyllis later discussed with Billy that a statistician's term for the most frequently occurring number was the "mode." At first Billy displayed the data about clutch size that was on the class chart but became dissatisfied because there wasn't enough variety in the ranges. He consulted the nest book and then included some vultures and hawks to give his graph more diversity. He made a chart of the range of numbers of eggs and found that the range of two was the most frequent. He was intrigued that six birds on his chart had no range, such as the hummingbird which always produced two eggs. As he shared all this information with Phyllis, she became interested in the findings and offered a theory to explain some of the data. When Billy showed her that 4 or 5 was the most "popular" number of eggs but that the vulture lays only two eggs, Phyllis hypothesized aloud that maybe large birds lay fewer eggs. Billy looked at his chart and they both considered the idea. Then Phyllis suddenly remembered that a hummingbird lays only two eggs. "I guess that theory won't work!" Billy chuckled. Phyllis was just as intrigued with this data as Billy was while they both sought to make some sense of what was displayed. Phyllis's willingness to offer her own theory was an important demonstration for Billy that it is alright to hypothesize on the best current data, knowing that it may need to be revised or abandoned as other data is revealed. The strategy of graphing was highlighting information that enabled us all to look more closely and conjecture about what seemed interesting. (See Appendix A for the self-evaluation form used at the conclusion of the nesting project.)

Drawing as a Tool for Understanding

Drawing also provided a unique perspective for looking closely at birds and other parts of the natural world. During the first week of school Eric brought a frog to class. During writing time he described his frog using both a narrative and a drawing. He was particularly intrigued with the color of the frog's eyes when it was under water. He told Phyllis that he did not have a crayon that matched the color he needed to show, and she helped him find a classmate who had a larger selection. The problem was solved, and when Eric shared his completed observation sheet with the class, both teacher and students praised him for the accuracy of his drawing. Eric's demonstration with precise artistic tools paralleled the lessons the class learned from Ashley's use of "peck" and Shunta's "greenish" in language.

As the children observed various birds throughout the year, many sketched or traced book illustrations. Shunta, for example, became particularly interested in cardinals, and soon the bulletin board was decorated with her cut-out sketches. One day Ashley, who had received a collection of feathers from her grandmother, commented to David, "I wonder if this feather is from a male or a female cardinal?" David asked her what had made her wonder about the feather. Ashley continued, "I got the idea off of the picture that Shunta drew." Ashley had been studying the shading of Shunta's drawing, and this experience gave her a new way of looking at her feathers.

Danny learned about bluebirds through drawing. When he showed the class a life-size bluebird that he had drawn, Phyllis asked him, "What did drawing the bluebird help you notice that you had not noticed before?" Danny answered that as he was drawing, he thought that bluebirds had very strong legs. He reached down to his own calf and described how the bluebird's leg looked as though it had muscles. The class then contributed ideas that substantiated Danny's hypothesis: The bluebirds could hang onto the hole in the birdhouse for long periods of time, and they perched easily on the electrical wire. The children compared the bluebird to the hummingbird, whose weak legs hang limply below its body in flight. A hummingbird's legs are so weak that it is easier to fly to reverse its position on a branch than it is to turn. Danny was interested in strength from a personal perspective as well. He was active in several sports teams and served as the sports co-anchor for the class news show. Drawing helped him connect what he knew about physical strength with what he was learning about birds.

It is interesting that in the course of scientific history drawing has been a vehicle to link perception and scientific theory. Galileo and an English astronomer, Thomas Harriot, used similar telescopes as they each studied the "strange spotted-nesse" of the moon (Edgerton, 1984). Two theories about the shadows prevailed at the time. One theory stated that the moon was made up of different substances that created the illusion of spots; the other described the moon as a gigantic mirror that reflected the earth's contours. Both theories were based on the religious belief that God would only create perfect, rather than rough, heavenly bodies. Influenced by these theories, Harriot's drawings looked like dotted flat disks. Galileo, on the other hand, had been trained as an artist as well as a scientist, and he had grown up in the rich artistic culture of Italy. His own personal training in chiaroscuro, or the rendering of light and shadow, influenced him to *see* differently. His artistic eye led him to draw the moon as a sphere with craters and mountains. His drawings enabled the scientific community to "see" differently, too, and the theories of the moon's composition changed radically.

Galileo used drawing to convey ideas that writing could not. In a similar way, Scott invented his own symbols to represent a visual/spatial observation: a bluebird's flight. When the bluebirds nested a dozen yards from our window, the children became fascinated watching them swoop from the electrical wire to the bluebird box, and then noting their flight pattern as they left the box. Scott studied the way they flapped their wings and glided, and he created a code of dashes to show this pattern (Fig 1-6). He described his code by saying, "This shows how many times it flapped or glided. I showed how it glided. The little dashes are for short glides; she glided a few feet, then she flapped again, and then she glided a few more feet. And the long is for she glided for a long time." Scott developed a unique way to represent movement in space on a two-dimensional plane; his lines show the pattern, direction, and chronology of the bluebird's flight. Rett appreciated the information that this visual conveyed: "It's neat how he drew it because it explains it more. Some people could just draw arrows but he shows *how* she's leaving the box. It's a little bit more specific." Scott's invention of the dashes yielded another layer of detail that Rett found intriguing. Art was a communicative tool that pushed us all to pay closer attention to the flight pattern of birds.

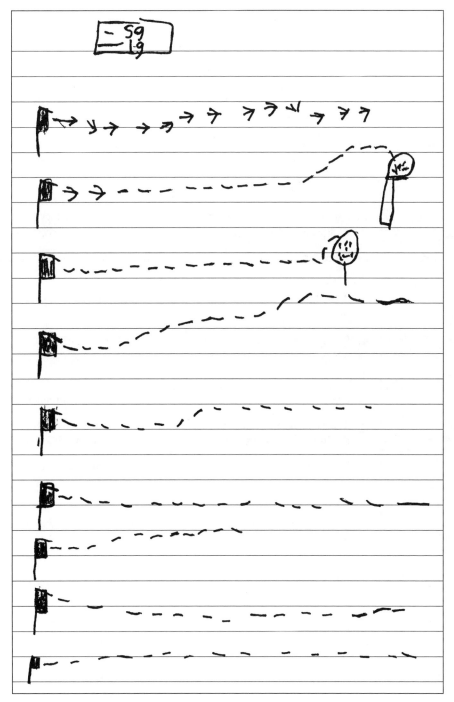

FIG 1–6 *Scott's Picture of Flight Patterns*

Developing a Cycle of Observing, Wondering, and Investigating

The class found early in the year that talking with the group generated possible extensions for their initial observations that sharpened their vision. Those first journal-sharing sessions set the tone of the spirit we were trying to foster. Table 1 shows examples of the range of observations and extensions from those early conversations:

Observations	*Extensions*
1. The hummingbirds looked like they were playing tag.	1. Do birds play tag? How and when do they communicate?
2. I didn't see any birds.	2. Where else do birds go? Which ones migrate? When?
3. A cardinal looked right at me. It was chewing	3. How do birds eat? How far can birds see?
4. I could see and hear birds everywhere.	4. What kind of noises do birds make? What do different noises mean?
5. I saw a cardinal on Scott's feeder.	5. Which birds prefer feeders? Why?
6. The cardinal went to a limb, then the grass, then Scott's feeder.	6. What is the movement pattern of birds around the feeders?
7. I saw a lot of house finches.	7. Do some birds travel in groups, while others come in pairs or alone?
8. Some birds did like the rain because a lot of them came.	8. How does weather affect birds?
9. I saw some birds scare off some other birds.	9. Are some birds enemies to other birds? Which birds are friends?

TABLE 1 *Developing a Cycle of Observing, Wondering, and Investigating*

As teachers and students raised questions, we all learned to look more closely. Our observations became connected day to day, and some of the themes that we pursued lasted for months. For several weeks no one saw any birds during the morning journal time, and the class journal was discontinued for awhile. During this period the class posed questions, such as did all the birds migrate, or did the later sunrise or colder temperatures affect bird behavior? Everyone watched for additional clues to the puzzle, and finally an employee at the local bird speciality store provided necessary information. Dogwood and other berries had ripened, and the birds were temporarily living from natural food sources. When the supplies were depleted, birds returned, and the students noticed new visitors.

Jonathan reported early in January that he saw six small birds on the ground, and they flew away. Rett helped to identify this new species as dark-eyed juncos. The class was intrigued with Jonathan's description because they had not seen birds move in large groups near the feeders, especially from the ground. Jenny wondered, "If they fly together, do they stick together, like are they family? If they're not family, do they fly back and forth together?" With these questions raised, the class began to watch flock behavior more closely. A few days later Rhiannon asked, "Why do birds, when they fly together, make so much noise?" thus connecting what we were observing with our eyes with our ears.

The class later learned the functions of bird calls and songs, and better appreciated communication in traveling flocks. After two more weeks of watching closely, Nikki told her classmates that "Juncos were in a big, huge ball when people got in line to go to PE, they all flew off in a ball, like they were protecting each other, like a huddle." Brent then theorized that maybe the adults were protecting the young as buffalo do: Adults get on the outside, and the young get on the inside. Again, over time the class learned from reading that some species have larger flocks in harsher climates in order to locate food supplies. Danielle—noticing how flocks of birds settled on branches of trees with regular spaces between birds—wondered if birds have "assigned seats." She asked a guest speaker from the Audubon Society, and he expanded upon her theory by explaining that most flocks have dominant members and a "pecking order." This cycle of observing, raising questions, generating theories, seeking information, and observing once again, enabled the children to appreciate the unique characteristics of various species of birds.

Extending the Cycle Over Time

Several of these initial observations were extended for most of the school year. For example, Rhiannon recorded an observation in the class journal on the first rainy morning of the year. When she shared her observation, several children wondered whether birds liked the rain or not. Shunta, referring to Rhiannon's report, remarked, "Some did like the rain because a lot of them came." Danielle commented that some birds like the rain because it's like a birdbath, but Scott objected because his pet bird once fell in a tub of water and was too waterlogged to fly. Phyllis, also caught up in the conversation, wondered aloud, "What about ducks?" Brent, who owned some ducks, described how they shake themselves when they come out of the water. Phyllis added that birds have oil on their feathers, and the children discussed that water birds might have more oil than birds that lived in the woods.

A few days later, the class revisited the ideas in this conversation, and Nicholas suggested an experiment design of dipping feathers from different birds in water. Volunteers collected feathers, and Amanda and Billy pursued a feather study for a focus project. Everyone was amazed when these children tried Nicholas's idea and dipped duck feathers in water; they felt completely dry when they were removed. Amanda and Billy learned that birds get oil from their diet, and they spread it from a special oil gland to their bodies during daily preening. Interest in feathers continued throughout the year as the class selected high oil-content bird seed and read about different species of birds. When the bluebirds established their territory in the school yard, the children observed the male's preening habits in detail. They were amazed to see him turn his head "almost completely around" to reach the oil gland at the base of his tail. They noticed also that he chose to perch high in the branches of a tree, where he could sit in the sun. The class theorized about this choice of location, and we finally found a section in a reference book that explained how oil in the feathers can produce Vitamin D in sunlight. Adding this new knowledge to her months of study, Amanda proudly narrated the section on preening in the class-authored video documentary of the bluebird family. As the class watched the completed video, we thought back to that rainy day when our wondering about feathers and rain had first begun.

Another cycle of observation, theorizing, reading, and more observation centered on the topic of bird communication. When Shunta read her journal aloud, she said that two hummingbirds looked like they were "playing tag." During the discussion that followed, the class wondered if birds do indeed play. It is important to note that no one said that Shunta was "wrong;" we were simply wondering collaboratively. A few days later when we were reading a nonfiction book about hummingbirds, we found some information that described how aggressive hummingbirds are, especially about their territory. This new information sharpened all of our vision as we observed more closely out the window. The children noticed over time more about bird communication, such as which species of birds drove others away, and which ones arrived at the feeders as a pair of a male and female. When the bluebirds arrived, the children (and adults) were puzzled to see the male flap his wing repeatedly with no intention of flying. Since the behavior was often linked with his preening, the children theorized that he was showing off. Again, a book gave us more information, and we read aloud that this phenomenon—called wing-waving—was another form of bird communication and bonding. With this knowledge, the class returned to the window, connecting theories of communication to the wonder of looking closely.

Models Extend the Cycle

Models also became tools not only for looking closely, but also for wondering and theorizing. When the class investigated nesting in March, Eric, Ashley, and Billy chose to create a life-size model of a bald eagle's nest. The dimensions were intriguing: an inner depression that measured 20 inches, and an overall diameter of five feet. When the children actually drew the nest on paper, their perspectives changed; they could really see the contrast between twenty inches and five feet more vividly. They borrowed two model bald eagle eggs from Chris's egg project (bald eagles lay clutches of two eggs) and laid them in the center. The two eggs looked lost in the nest, and the children and Phyllis gathered around the model together. This amazement, born in the act of looking closely, led the children to extend their investigation in two ways. First, Billy commented that the bald eagle's egg was about the size of a hummingbird's nest. Inspired by his comparison, the group spent the next day estimating how many hummingbird eggs could fit in the eagle's nest. It was the model that provided the basis for this interesting comparison.

Eric inspired a second extension as he studied the model. He mused, "I have a wonder. I wonder how come they have so much room on the outside (the large space between the center depression and the edge of the nest), 'cause this is how much is on the inside. I mean, why would they have so much? So they could spot it? Like see it real good from high in the air, 'cause, you know, how they fly real high, and they could take food to the babies." Ashley offered a second theory that was related to feeding. She hypothesized that the large outer rim could serve as a meal tray when the adults brought prey. Billy decided that the nest had to be big enough for both adult eagles and their active offspring. When the children read a pamphlet that Ashley brought to school, they found that indeed the adults did deposit the food there and the young eagles used the rim for exercise. The group could appreciate this written account more fully because they had developed their own theories for the nest's function.

Theories Lead to Understanding the Interconnectedness of the Natural World

Looking closely, whether it was through direct observation or through the support of tools, was merely a beginning point for speculation. Over the year the members of this class learned to raise questions and to entertain multiple theories that addressed those questions. They knew that with the collaborative power of the group, they would get support for some of their ideas, but they also realized that the cycle of observation, wondering, and further investigation was never ending.

When the class looked closely at the wonder of the natural world, it became impossible to separate one part of nature from another. When the children wondered about weather, their investigations led to diet, vegetation, and health. For instance, the children discovered that sunlight converted the oil in birds' feathers to vitamin D; they also found that when the weather became cooler, certain berries ripened to provide birds with another important source of food. Discussions about communication led to a better understanding of territorial and habitat needs of a variety of creatures. For example, the children learned that bluebird boxes needed to be spaced 100 yards apart from each other to support an adequate supply of insects for each set of young birds. The children also heard the loud squawking of certain birds that drove off competitors from the yard in order to protect their territory. These insights helped the children better understand the interconnectedness of the natural world. A guest speaker from the Audubon Society also emphasized this same idea. He commented that once he started looking closely at birds, he started looking closely at other parts of the natural world, such as trees, flowers, insects, land forms, climate, and so forth. For our class, watching birds provided a natural avenue for seeing the interconnectedness of the world. What counts in inquiry, then, is not the particular subject, but the initial interest, followed by a sustained period of observing, sharing those descriptions together, and generating wonders and theories collaboratively. Any aspect of nature will demonstrate the web of connections that exist in the natural world.

A Final Reflection

We have found that looking closely is no simple matter, though science textbooks and curricular guidelines may portray it otherwise. It is often deemed a "lower level skill" that requires little analysis or reflection. However, we have found such thinking to be misguided. Our work has shown us that looking closely is grounded in an ongoing sense of wonder about what is occurring in the natural world, such as how do birds communicate, and why do the same birds travel in groups. Looking closely involves realizing the limits of one's vision, such as the children knowing that what they were seeing outside the window was only part of the story. Looking closely means acknowledging what is not seen, such as the kind of birds that did *not* appear at the feeder, and considering that data as also valuable. Looking closely involves grappling with the problems of scientists, such as devising a strategy for watching the birds when everything happens so quickly. Lastly, looking closely is an activity for making personal connections, such as William's describing a bluebird that guards its home like a soldier. Looking closely is not a skill that we outgrow but one that all learners continually refine as they gain new experiences in varied contexts.

2

Inquiry Demands a Critical Use of Resources

Inquirers are doubters. They look at the world with a skeptical eye. In this chapter we document how the children became critical readers of a wide range of resources: field guides, general reference books, pictures, maps, letters from relatives, interviews, newsletters, student-authored texts, adult textbooks, poetry, fiction, and even the labels on a bag of birdseed. Children used these resources to raise questions, make personal connections, and construct theories. They found that specialized resources have both benefits and limitations. For example, they learned that range maps show population distribution, but not density. They also gained important insights about the writing process because they were critical readers and writers themselves

Gathering Resources Naturally

We did not have any books about birds in the classroom for the first week or two of school, and as we look back on it, we are happy about that choice. Our learning began at the window, where we first observed hummingbirds. Those little marvels fascinated the children with their speed of flight, their ability to hover, and their delicate use of their long, slender beaks. Rhiannon, our second observer, counted one hummingbird taking seventeen sips at the feeder. Her classmates' comments raised questions about how a hummingbird actually sipped and why it ate so much at one visit to the feeder. Reflecting this need for more information, the first books we borrowed from the library were mostly nonfiction picture books about hummingbirds. Many children read the books during silent reading and wrote about them during writing time.

On other occasions we read selected parts aloud, highlighting current areas of interest. For example, we read that each second of a hummingbird's sip is really composed of thirteen kittenlike laps. The class was amazed at this fact. A few days later, when Amanda wrote that a hummingbird took about fifty sips, the class insisted upon calculating the total number of laps: 650. We were learning one of our first lessons about resources: Observation led us to books, and the books led us back to the window. Months later, when we spoke with naturalist Rudy Mancke, he confirmed our own experience:

> Usually it's the experience [observation] that makes you want to know more. It just so happened that in my life that's the way it worked. I had the experiences. I wanted the information. Then I found the library. Then all of a sudden it was the most wonderful kind of marriage that could be. I just have never stopped. (1995)

Seeking resources grew out of a specific need, and the need came from direct observation and wonder. Our use of field guides followed the same pattern. When the class questioned Rhiannon about the color of the hummingbird that she saw, Scott extended the conversation by describing the color differences between many male and female birds. In the days that followed, Scott continued to contribute information about species that he had learned at home. Finally one morning Scott appeared, struggling with a heavy book bag. "Look what I brought the class," he beamed. Unzipping his bag, he revealed a dictionary-sized field guide, already marked in several places. Instead of bringing in his knowledge from home bit by bit, he was now sharing a larger source. In this way he was adding to the credibility of his contributions ("Here's proof. It's right here."), and he was inviting the class to follow his lead in seeking information. Within days Scott's guide was filled with Post-it notes, and Scott was teaching his classmates how to look up species and read range maps. We were building a community of inquirers where learners sought resources through personal investment, and where everyone was capable of leading each other. As with all good learning, we as teachers were also learning along the way, and the children helped forge the best lessons.

Learning to Think Critically

Now that the class was consulting written resources regularly, we noticed a new problem. When the students chose to "research" during writing time, they furiously copied large sections of text into their notebooks. Fascinated as they were with the information, they were not combining it with any observations or information from other sources. We decided that a minilesson on note taking based on Donald Graves's *Investigate Nonfiction* (1989) would encourage the children to develop a personal voice in writing nonfiction. However, we were not prepared for the lesson they were to teach us.

We borrowed one set of Ashley's "notes," a copied description of blue jays. Phyllis read each sentence of the article aloud to the class and asked volunteers to describe what they had heard. She recorded their ideas in note form on an over-head transparency. For example, the passage described the jay as "a sentry of the forest" who warns of "approaching danger with its raucous, jeering 'jeeah'." Jonathan suggested that the sentence told us that blue jays "warn other birds of a big thing coming. Other birds fly off." Phyllis recorded Jonathan's ideas and continued reading a sentence that described the jay's habitat. Tony simplified the description of "coniferous woodlands and pine forests," by saying that the jay lives in forests, and Billy added, "pine forests." This comment gave the class the opportunity to tie the word *coniferous* to the word *cone*. Finally, the children analyzed a sentence describing the jay's behavior as "aggressive" when it defended its nesting territory. Rett recognized the word *aggressive* and explained that the bird was very brave, even a bully, and that other birds wouldn't try to pick on jays. Phyllis recorded these last interpretations on the overhead, lay the pen down, and prepared to summarize the main points of the minilesson. In her mind, the minilesson was successful and complete because the children had interpreted the main ideas of the article in familiar language. However, Shawn showed that the lesson was hardly over when he asked, "Why would a bully help other birds?"

His question caught Phyllis by surprise. The real point of the lesson probably was not how to take notes at all. Shawn was showing us all that inquirers must be critical and analytical when they read pieces of nonfiction. The class had established a norm of questioning each other's observations ("How did you know it was the same bird?" "How do you know that it took seventeen sips?"). Now Shawn was approaching an "authoritative" book with this same sense of skepticism. The real minilesson, the one from the children's agenda, was now the one that Phyllis knew she had to address.

She replied, "That's what scientists do. They question and wonder about what they read. When you read and research, it's important to do what Shawn has done. Does anyone have a theory about Shawn's idea, why a bully might be able to help other birds?" Several children contributed:

Eric: Maybe blue jays really care for other birds.
Rett: Maybe they're just protecting themselves. They don't mean to help other birds.
Ashley: If they're so big and pretty, maybe their colors help warn other birds.
Danielle: Maybe blue jays care about *some* birds.
Billy: Maybe they warn other birds because *they* are scared.
Shunta: Maybe they're scared and not as brave with people.
Kevin: Why do blue jays sometimes act nice toward cardinals?

By contributing hypotheses about these two contrasting ideas in the article, the rest of the class joined with Shawn in reading the article critically. Eric chose to reject the validity of the aggressive description, while Rett debated the idea of their being friendly. Their ideas, as well as Billy's, underscored the fact that humans can only observe and describe animal behavior: They cannot interview birds to find out how they feel. Ashley used additional information from the article about color and size to reconcile the difference. Danielle and Shunta questioned that perhaps the article was not specific enough; additional details could clarify the situation. Kevin's comment brought the class back to our own observations at the window. His information about the behavior of blue jays gave support to some of his classmate's theories about how a blue jay could be both kind and aggressive. As the class concluded the discussion, they all realized that reading an article was not an "end" to a question, but a beginning point for a new cycle of questioning.

Encouraging Different Interpretations

This discussion also showed that creating a range of interpretations about a given phenomenon is an important activity within a community of scientists. Recently some geologists renewed the debate over how the dinosaurs perished (McDonald, 1993, pp. 6–7, 13); they claim they have evidence to show that a Mexican crater believed to be the site of a massive meteorite impact is nearly twice as large as originally measured. Some argue that these new measurements, if confirmed, would support the theory that dinosaurs became extinct from this cataclysmic collision, which blocked sunlight and cooled the earth in a global "nuclear winter." Other scientists disagree with the findings. Some argue that the crater is much smaller and challenge the model that was used to calculate these larger dimensions. Other paleontologists remain unconvinced because many kinds of life, such as turtles and alligators, survived. These species should have been more susceptible to acid rain, which was created by the debris from the collision. Living in a collaborative, scientific community means entertaining these various interpretations. The children, like these scientists, were seeing how people could take a different slant on a given situation.

Developing Healthy Skepticism

Chris taught us another lesson, when he, like Kevin, compared his personal experience with the information in a book. He borrowed an old field guide from the library, and as he was reading about the species that visited our feeders, he found a puzzling piece of information. Literally dozens of house finches had visited the feeders, easily recognized by the photographs in our class bird guides. In the library guide, however, Chris found that the habitat map for the house finch located this species only along the west coast. He brought his problem to a class meeting. We checked the publishing dates: 1949, 1956. We suggested that a volunteer might consult one of our other class guides that was published recently. The habitat map in the newer guide showed the finch's range as covering both the west coast and much of the eastern half of the country. The accompanying text supplied the answer. The house finch was native to the west coast, but during the 1940s some people brought pairs of finches in cages to Long Island to sell. Fearful when they learned what they had done was illegal, they released them. In the following decades the finches multiplied and spread north and south. Today they are one of the most frequent visitors to home feeders in all states in the eastern regions of our country.

Chris had shown the class another unanticipated lesson in reading nonfiction. The discrepancy between the two texts highlighted that science changes, and that any nonfiction work reflects the context in which it was written. Through demonstrations such as Chris's and Shawn's the students were coming to realize that even facts and theories are only tentative best guesses. The class was developing a spirit of healthy skepticism that made them unwilling to accept "facts" at face value. Months later, when the owner of the local bird store, Mr. Kelly, visited the class, he shared a similar story. After a bad winter storm, he had once seen spots of blue on the snow. At first glance he presumed them to be bluebirds, but with the aid of binoculars he knew they were not. Checking his field guide, he identified the birds as lazuli buntings, which were not supposed to be found in the eastern portion of the U.S. He called the Audubon Society, and a representative came to his house, confirming his identification. Perhaps these visitors were affected by weather patterns, but, whatever the reason, his field guide simply did not match what he was seeing. Mr. Kelly, like the fourth graders, knew the importance of checking one's experience against printed information and questioning that information if it seemed anomalous. By his sharing his story, he was showing the children that they were not only learning science, but they were thinking like scientists.

Interpreting range maps raised another issue in January. After studying these maps in some newly acquired books, William shared an idea with the class. "I wonder if we could figure out what bird has the most population?"

Nicholas, who quickly flipped through a guide on his desk, raised his hand. "It's the evening grosbeak and the crow."

"How did you decide?" Phyllis asked.

He held up a range map and pointed. "They are colored in the most."

Eric raised his hand in protest. "A large area doesn't mean that there are a lot of birds." In his own way, Eric was trying to distinguish between area and density, and the class spent part of our meeting time exploring this distinction. Later that month the school held its annual social studies fair, and Ashley created a poster of maps showing ranges of well-known American birds, which she shared with the class. Actually seeing these colorful maps side by side led the students to analyze the distinction between area and density more closely. One of the maps showed the bald eagle's range stretching from coast to coast. The blue jay's range, on the other hand, was confined to the area east of the Rockies. The students knew from their reading and experience that blue jays far outnumber bald eagles. Drawing upon this knowledge, Ashley's visual display, and our earlier conversation, they could make sense of the mathematical concepts of area and density (number of birds per square mile.) This incident reminded us again of one of the benefits of a long-term study. When children have opportunities to revisit a concept in a new context, they are able to combine resources in a new way. Learners only become flexible users of resources when they are given the time to do so.

The Power of Story in Nonfiction Texts

We learned another unanticipated lesson about the role of resources through our own involvement with reading. While reading a children's book about egrets, we learned that cattle egrets have a mysterious history. They are actually an African species that were first spotted in the United States in 1952 by amateurs, who found them following cattle in Florida. The amateurs could not identify these strange birds, so they took pictures of them. When they made the photographs public, pieces of the puzzle surfaced. People in South America indicated that cattle egrets had first been established there, but this information did not explain the underlying question of how the birds crossed the Atlantic Ocean.

Fascinated by this unsolved mystery, we shared the story with the class. As always, the children were ready to contribute theories. Scott volunteered that the egrets may have come on a ship by accident. Billy added, "Maybe a storm wrecked their nest, and they got lost in the rain." Danny extended the conversation by trying to figure out not only how the birds got to South America, but also how they survived upon arrival. He pointed to our world map and commented that parts of Africa lay along "the same lines" (latitude lines) as part of South America. "Maybe the weather was about the same because it matched, and the birds were comfortable in the new place."

It was not until much later that we realized the significance of this conversation from the point of view of an attitude toward resources. Readers of fiction become involved with a text through identifying with the plights of characters, enjoying the excitement or poignancy of plot, and by predicting events as they read. They are transported to another place and time through the act of reading (Rosenblatt, 1978). Traditionally, readers of nonfiction have been viewed as more detached; they are looking for information. Through experiences like the cattle egret story, we developed a broader view of what it means to read nonfiction from an inquiry perspective. Nonfiction, too, is full of story, and we are transported toanother time and place in a different way. Readers can become involved emotionally by sharing the wonder, awe, and mystery of the story, and from actively participating in theory building alongside established scientists in the field. Rudy Mancke (1995) likened being a naturalist to reading Sherlock Holmes; both solve mysteries by examining evidence and generating theories. Reading nonfiction, then, becomes an invitation to investigate the deepest stories of humankind.

We also realized an aspect of the teacher's role in developing this inquiring stance toward resources. As on many other occasions, we were genuinely interested in the mystery of the cattle egret. We shared the story and invited theories because of our own excitement. When we looked back, we realized this sharing was an un-planned but powerful lesson to the children. We had shown the class our own process of becoming involved with a nonfiction text, and by doing so, we invited the children to follow our lead. Without realizing it, we had acted as mentors of reading. This lesson helped us seek future opportunities to demonstrate this stance. Once again we had learned about the process by being immersed in it.

When we reflected upon the lessons that grew from the natural questions raised by Shawn, Chris, William, Ashley, and others, we realized that our class was developing a characteristic stance toward resources. A critical user of resources raises questions by comparing and contrasting information within a text, such as the apparent inconsistency of an aggressive blue jay that helps its fellow birds. Active users of resources compare their personal experience with information in books, like Chris with his observation of house finches. A critical reader raises the question, "But the resource *doesn't* say . . .", as Eric pointed out when Nicholas assumed that a wide range indicated a high population of birds. Finally, we learned that the underlying stance toward reading nonfiction is more like our attitude toward fiction than we would have anticipated. When learners seek information based on questions rooted in wonder, they read with wonder. By joining their observations, theories, and stories with those of the larger community of scientists, these readers, too, are transported to another place and time.

Searching for Multiple Resources

At first the children regarded books as the only location "where you looked things up." When we did not have a book in the room that addressed a current question, they fell back on the most obvious source of all, the encyclopedia. In the fall when the children noticed mockingbirds in the school yard, Ashley and Deidre visited the library and printed an entry from the school's computerized encyclopedia. Although this information was interesting, it was limited. Through multiple experiences over time, however, the children discovered a wide variety of resources: pictures, maps, letters, interviews, models, student-authored texts, labels on products, adult textbooks, poetry, and fiction.

Models as Resources

One fall day Rhiannon surprised the class with a gift. She and her mother had found a set of life-size bird models that could be hung from the ceiling. That afternoon Rhiannon and a friend assembled the colorful cardboard birds, and we arranged them above the groups of desks. These models became a "hanging field guide" of sorts, almost seeming to fly on the air currents in the room. We found that one of the values of models was that they give a three-dimensional perspective that pictures lack. Many of our field guides only illustrated birds from one angle, whereas the models showed all sides of the bird at once. Having the models be actual size was a convenient feature: It was easy to compare the size and shape of a bluebird and a blue jay by glancing overhead. Often students referred to these models in order to identify a new species that they observed at the window, even if a specific species was not represented by a cardboard bird. Danny once pointed to the model flicker and cardinal saying, "The bird I saw was about as big as those two birds combined." The models thus became a handy reference to encourage description, confirm identification, and to study unique features of species.

People as Resources

The class learned other lessons about seeking resources when they needed to make decisions about what birdseed varieties to purchase. At the beginning of the year, the children used some inexpensive seed mix bought at a grocery store to fill the feeder. We knew that more specialized mixes were available, but until we were successful in attracting birds, we didn't want to make the investment. However, as the birds began to populate the feeders, the class noticed the ground littered with unused seed. When the initial bag of seed was almost depleted, we invited students to meet us at Mr. Kelly's bird specialty shop that Saturday.

Our Saturday meeting became our first lesson in interviewing experts as resources. Ashley and Jenny were the two students who were able to meet us at the store, and they described our concern about wasted seed to Mr. Kelly. He showed the girls various kinds of seed, explaining that "grocery store seed" contains at least 50 percent milo, which is primarily a filler. He said that birds toss milo onto the ground as they search for the seeds of their choice. Sunflower seeds are the most popular because they are rich in oil, which birds need for energy and for their feathers. Ashley studied the milo and confirmed that this variety matched the discarded seed below our feeder. (She was playing the role of a detective by matching the evidence!) The girls decided to purchase a seed with high sunflower content and with no milo. Not only had the girls learned about seed preference and nutrition, but they also learned that experts in the field are informative nonfiction resources to consult.

Mr. Kelly taught the girls another lesson about evaluating information during our visit. Although birds in the East discard milo, some western birds prefer it. His comment led Jenny to hypothesize that perhaps the manufacturers of grocery store seed included milo because they "didn't know where the seed would be used," arguing that birdseed was probably mass-produced. Perhaps Jenny was basing part of her hypothesis upon the fact that she knew that many grocery stores are chains, whereas Mr. Kelly's shop was a specialty store. Jenny shared this information with the class and explained her hypothesis. A month later Rhiannon conducted an indepth study of the types of seeds most liked by various species. Her reading, which listed several species that preferred milo over other seed, extended Mr. Kelly's information. Once again we all realized that no "fact," such as "Milo is filler seed" could be clearly labeled as absolute; in one context milo was used as a filler, but in another context it was a preferred choice. The class revisited this complex issue once again in March, when the Cornell Laboratory of Ornithology sent us some materials. An article reported that even within the same species, birds at the western part of the range would eat milo more readily than those of the exact species in the eastern area (Rosenberg and Dhondt, 1995). We all had learned that even a bag of seed needed to be viewed as a text to be considered critically from different perspectives.

During our visit Mr. Kelly suggested the names of other bird experts in the community, and we arranged for several guest speakers. These speakers helped the class learn more about birds as well as more about what it means to be a scientist. Billy highlighted for the class that *people's* information, like information in books, needs to be compared and questioned. A month or so after we set up a bluebird house, Billy and some of his classmates observed a chickadee investigating the box. Billy was worried; he knew that some species of birds harm others, but he had no information about chickadees as harmful. When the class wrote letters to Cornell, Billy asked for help in this matter. While waiting for a reply, a woman from the local wildlife rescue organization spent a morning talking with the class. Billy asked her about his concern. She replied that chickadees "are pretty shy" and not to worry about the bluebirds' safety. Although we felt reassured, Billy apparently was not completely satisfied with her answer. Two weeks later we invited the president of our Audubon Society chapter to speak to the class. On the day before his talk, the class brainstormed questions to ask him. Billy raised his hand. "I'm going to ask Mr. Dennis about the chickadees," he said boldly. "I want to see if he answers it the same way." Billy's comment showed us all once again that scientists are like detectives; they constantly weigh evidence from different sources, even human ones. After Mr. Dennis gave the same answer, Billy was finally satisfied.

Mr. Dennis indeed shared valuable information with the class when he visited the next day. He imitated bird calls, invited the kids to look through his spotting scope, explained the problem of forest fragmentation (see Chapter 4), showed how he kept notes in his field guide, and described numerous species and their habitats. After an hour and a half of discussion he taught the class another lesson when he remarked, "I'm only a beginner." Some children gasped, as their eyes met each other in amazement. Mr. Dennis, noting their reactions, explained that the more he learned, the more he realized that he wanted to know. In his talk he had described many unsolved mysteries and unanswered questions. He had demonstrated that all the resources in the world can never put an end to inquiry. It is this humble stance of an inquiring mind that makes a scientist open to new perspectives and responsive to new ideas. The natural world changes, even in twenty-four hours (Mancke, 1995), so there are always new relationships to consider. Mr. Dennis, however, was not the least bit discouraged by his confession of limited knowledge. He clearly was joyful in his continued inquiry. He welcomed unanswered questions and new paths to follow.

FIG 2–1   *Shunta and Rhiannon Using the Spotting Scope*

Friends and Family as Resources

The class found people to be resources in other ways as well. In October the students developed areas of interest to explore and present as projects. Nikki was interested in birds that eat on the ground, while Danielle, Scott, and Ashley wanted to learn more about the seed preference of certain species. Although these students used books, they found our class journal was another handy reference. The journal had an added advantage because reading could be easily followed by an interview with the author. In this way the children began to see that our own documentation was an authentic and useful nonfiction resource.

Letter writing extended our community of human resources in still another way. Ashley wrote her grandmother in Ohio, asking about the species she found at her feeders (see Chapter 5). They became regular correspondents, and in April her grandmother sent a collection of five huge scrapbooks, in which she had collected newspaper articles, kept lists of species, dates, and locations, and pages of a wide variety of feathers. The scrapbooks were her legacy of years of meticulous record keeping in the 1950s and 1960s. She had been wondering who would be interested in them, and through her correspondence with Ashley, she found a trusted home for her treasures. Ashley brought the scrapbooks to school, and her classmates pored over them during reading time. These scrapbooks, like our class journal and our bluebird graphs, helped the class see and appreciate the role of the amateur in documenting natural history. Science and research became less distant; everyone was invited to participate. Ashley's mother wrote at the close of the school year:

> Ashley has always gone to her Grandmother's bird feeder with her. They would watch the birds swarm to the feeders. It seems that now the two of them have a very unique common love. They talk about the different types of birds and feathers. Her Grandmother sent scrapbook journals filled with daily data on her bird watching, feathers, and articles, etc. that were over thirty years old. It is so unique how the two generations have shared their feelings.

Research is hardly a cold and detached process. We build friends by sharing resources, and our resources become our friends.

Fiction as a Resource

Our study of birds blurred the lines between nonfiction, poetry, and fiction, both as readers and writers. In October we decided to read aloud *The Trumpet of the Swan* (White, 1970). We had loved reading this story to our family as well as to previous classes, and we appreciated its portrayal of a boy who kept a journal and recorded his "wonders." We were not prepared, however, for its impact on both the class and on us. We were not the readers we had been; we were seeing this story with fresh eyes.

One of the ways that the class was first impressed with the book was through the author's style and word choice. E.B. White faced similar issues as the class did in describing birds' actions. We all noticed right away his careful choice of verbs, such as *glided*, *stretched*, *gazed*, and *twisted*. After reading a chapter, we discussed White's word choice with the class. They, too, had tackled the problem of conveying meaning through careful word choice, as recalled by the conversations about *peck* and *greenish* (see Chapter 1). The class appreciated the author's skill from the point of view of fellow naturalists.

Next we all noticed facts. Even though we adults had read the book numerous times, these sentences came to life in a new way when we were preparing for the next day's reading:

> The male stretched out his great wings, eight feet from tip to tip, and gave the water a mighty clout to show his strength. This made him feel better right away. When a Trumpeter Swan hits an enemy with his wing, it is like being hit by a baseball bat. (White, 1970:, p. 12)

Eight feet! That's HUGE! Mentally we envisioned this wing span: a six-foot tall human, but then add width . . . The class had been watching ruby-throated hummingbirds from the window all fall, and they had learned that six of them weighed as much as a chickadee. How great the trumpeter swan seemed after our recent experience of looking closely. The children spent some time imagining these large dimensions. Excited by the conversation, after school we constructed a model eight-foot wing span from paper and tacked it to the ceiling above the rug where we read. During the rest of the book, everyone would gaze at those huge wings from time to time as we read, and even after we finished, we left the model up to remind us of these amazing birds.

Tying Fiction and Nonfiction Together as Readers

The passage caused us to reflect upon authorship in other ways as well, and we shared our insights with the children. White had used an exact measurement, obviously drawn from research, without sounding detached or overly scientific. He conveyed his knowledge through the medium of story. White was showing us about the role of story in new ways: Story is perhaps the foundation of all our communication of knowledge.

White also used metaphorical images to describe his scientific knowledge: Being hit by a swan is compared to being hit by a baseball bat. When we read this sentence aloud, several children gasped. Everyone knows how hard a baseball bat can swing; a few of us know from unhappy personal experiences. Even though none of us in the class had seen a trumpeter swan, we all could imagine the power of its wings through White's imagery. Metaphorical images transcend place and time, as evidenced by a parallel story from the history of geology. Mt. Vesuvius erupted in 79 A.D., but people even today can picture its explosion by reading Pliny's written record:

> A cloud, from which mountain was uncertain, at this distance, was ascending, the appearance of which I cannot give you a more exact description than by likening it to that of a pine tree, for it shot up to a great height in the form of a very tall trunk, which spread itself out at the top into a sort of branches; occasioned, I imagine, either by a sudden gust of air that impelled it, the force of which decreased as it advanced upwards, or the cloud itself being pressed back

again by its own weight, expanded in the manner I have mentioned, it appeared sometimes bright and sometimes dark and spotted, according as it was more or less impregnated with earth and cinders. (Harrington, 1994, p. 10)

Almost two thousand years later, readers can see that terrible cloud because they, too, know pine trees. Scientists need to be skilled writers.

White's analogy also allows readers to marvel at the uniqueness of this powerful bird, just as Pliny's description of the massive volcanic cloud evokes awe. Metaphorical images and poetic language enable readers to see more vividly and feel more deeply. Rett further demonstrated this point when he told us about a favorite passage from a nonfiction book that described the plight of bluebirds: "It's (knowing bluebirds) like a memory, not a reality." In his reading Rett learned that the bluebird population fell drastically after house sparrows and starlings were brought to the United States from England. The words which the author used to convey this sad fact touched Rett's heart, not just his mind.

Finally, this short passage by E. B. White showed us that writers use fiction to explain the spaces that observations cannot verify. White describes the cob's feelings upon striking the water. Of course people cannot really know how a trumpeter swan feels when it shows its strength. Humans use fiction—poetry, story, myth—to fill in these spaces they long to know more about. As we read this sentence to ourselves, we thought of Cortney, who had recently told us that for her focused study she wanted to learn more about "how birds feel." We had originally felt uncomfortable with calling Cortney's topic scientific: How could she document feelings? When we read *The Trumpet of the Swan*, we better appreciated Cortney's wish. She and White shared an author's perspective. White had studied swans carefully. He had done his research, but all this work still left him wondering. The edges of fiction overlap with those of nonfiction, for White, Cortney, and all of us.

Rudy Mancke (1995) explained the perspective of fiction and its benefits for the scientist in another way. We discussed with him the fact that many of science's great breakthroughs in inventions and theories have been made by people who were new to their field, or even outside their field. In his reply to our query about this pattern, he explained the importance of a scientist's developing multiple perspectives:

[People new to the field] haven't got blinders on. The worst thing in the world you can do—and I say this to myself a lot—asking questions is wonderful, but you have to get your perspectives changed, and that's true for everybody. You have to look at the world from somebody else's viewpoint. When I was teaching I used to talk about that a lot. What is life like for the Eastern Box Turtle? What's a long distance for a box turtle? How long are you living? How much of a distance do you cover in your life? Why? What kind of habitat are you going to live in? Can you live in a really grown-up area? You probably couldn't even move through a grown-up area. You've got enough trouble with that shell on anyway. So that affects where you live. It all works together. Get your perspectives changed a little bit. I do that all the time. I'm a ravenous reader. I read all sorts of areas, and I'm better for every one of them.

Box turtles can't talk. In order to understand their perspective, people can pretend they're turtles. Fiction helps change perspectives on our knowing. By filling in the spaces of our knowledge with story, people learn to appreciate the natural world from the inside out. By comparing our feelings with those of natural creatures, we develop a new sense of respect and care for their well-being. Changing perspectives leads us back to wonder in new ways.

This changed perspective also helped the class make connections with social studies. At the time the class was studying the Mountain West region, in which the book was set. The swans in the story left their breeding grounds in Canada to winter in the Red Rock Lakes of Montana. White described from the swans' point of view the ideal conditions of these unusual lakes. They are fed with hot springs, so they do not freeze even when snow piles deep on the shore. Again the perspective of the swans' needs for survival helped the class better appreciate the connections between geography and wildlife.

On the day when we finished the book, several of the students' comments revealed the blend of fiction and nonfiction once more. White described the swans flying at 10,000 feet. Assuming that the statement was accurate, we calculated the distance in miles so that we could visualize and appreciate it more fully. When we read that two swans took a dip in a hotel bathtub, Shunta objected that they might not fit. Eric reached for his field guide and located a description of a mute swan. He read aloud that a mute swan (the species he could locate) is 40" long. We realized that the fit would indeed be tight, and the birds must not have opened their wings! Even in this obvious fictitious setting, the class used a nonfiction resource to better imagine this exaggerated scene. Next, David shared a current question of his, "How many birds return to their place of birth?" He took an aspect of the story that he knew was true, and opened the possibility of investigating this habit in other species. Shunta worried about the feelings of a mother swan: "I wonder if Serena minds when Louis gave the cygnets away?" Finally, Jenny led us back to an author's perspective when she remarked, "Did he [White] get to see trumpeter swans?" Despite the obvious fictitious parts of the book, such as Louis learning to write, Jenny knew that an author of fiction, like an author of scientific observation, needs to know the topic well. Fiction embodies fact, fact embodies fiction, and both are rooted in wonder and story.

Tying Fiction and Nonfiction Together as Writers

Reading *The Trumpet of the Swan* and reciting numerous poems about birds influenced the children's writing. Creating stories and poems about birds enabled the students to claim their knowledge in new ways. The day after we finished *The Trumpet of the Swan*, Eric and Shawn worked together during writing time. Eric had previously written and illustrated several comics, which he read aloud to the class to everyone's delight. On this day Eric invited Shawn to co-author a comic. They were sketching to generate ideas when Shawn suggested, "Why don't we make a comic about birds?" Their resulting story shows the influence of the novel:

Last Action Swan

One day a swan was swimming on the lake and a fox was taking a walk. He came upon a big brown nest. Inside he saw four eggs. He was real hungry, so he took an egg. When the swan returned she saw only three eggs.

The next day the swan went out for her daily swim, and a raccoon was walking around the lake. The raccoon came upon the nest. The swan saw the raccoon, she swam as fast as she could to the shore, when she reached the nest she was too late. Only two eggs were left.

The next day she didn't go for a swim. Instead she stayed to protect her nest. Underneath her was a rat. The rat popped out of his hole and saw the eggs, it was about lunch time so he took an egg. Ten minutes later the swan looked under her and saw one egg left.

The next day the swan hid her egg in a different part of her nest, and went for a swim. The raccoon went to see if an egg was still there. ALL RIGHT! There's one more egg left all the animals that took an egg came to the nest. The swan heard the noise she turned her back to look at her nest. She swam across the lake and on the shore. When she got to her nest she whacked the animals, and looked in her nest. The last egg was gone. She turned her head and saw the rat with something white on his back, quickly she pecked him with hard beak. The egg was saved.

Information About Swans

The swan's wing span is eight feet across. The nest is six feet across. The sound of a swan is louder than a trumpet. Long ago there were only around sixty-five left in the world.

The boys read their comic to the class, and several students complimented them on the suspense of the story, the inclusion of "information about swans," and the happy ending. Then Brent raised his hand and asked, "Why did they build a nest on land, and not toward the lake?"

Eric replied, "It really is a grassy area. We didn't draw in all the grass."

Brent's question demonstrated that the students regarded student-authored texts in similar ways to professionally authored ones. When we read *The Trumpet of the Swan*, we checked many of the scientific details (wing span, nest size, habitat, migration pattern) with other nonfiction sources. We respected White for his research. Brent was concerned that the boys' comic might not be portraying the swans' nest accurately. White had explained the selection of the nest site carefully, showing its importance for protection from predators. Even though the plot was fiction, these readers wanted the details to reflect accurate research.

Eric and Shawn, pleased with their success, authored a second comic that described a fight between two male cardinals over one female. Before long other children followed their lead and wrote comics, fables, and short stories that featured birds as characters. Some, such as Shunta's story, "Cardinals in Love," reflected knowledge from reading or observations. Shunta had noticed that some birds left the feeder when house finches arrived, but cardinals stayed, so in her story the cardinal talked to "his friends" the finches. Other students relied less on specific details about birds in their stories. They showed their knowledge of birds by being able to name many species. Rett's poem is an example:

Birds in My House

There is a pigeon in my room
A vulture on my head
Then I walked in the kitchen
and saw a dove on the bread.
Why do birds like my house? I wonder why
A mockingbird in the living room
A blue jay in the sky
There is an eagle in the den
wrestling with a hen
The hen went down for a pin
one, two, three
the hen broke its knee
That is all the birds in my house
Just about at least,
Did I mention that I was a little tiny chickadee?

Other pieces of children's work showed us that even a piece intended as nonfiction can sometimes blend into the realm of story and myth. When the students gathered data about the bluebirds' nesting (Chapter 4), Lily created a graph showing how long the male and female birds stayed in the box when they brought food for the nestlings. She wrote a commentary to explain her interpretation of the data:

The longest the male was in the box was thirty secs. I wonder what it was doing. The largest the female has went in the box was nine times. The male went in six times. When the female went in the box it stop for the night and went to sleep. I think the male goes back and gets some more food and then goes to the box and feed the babies and watches the nest for no predator will come like the sparrow who kills baby bluebirds. And the female. I wonder why it kills the babies and the female. I think a long time ago the bluebirds did something to the sparrows. Like for they will have a fight. Maybe because the sparrow wants the bluebirds nest. I wonder that.

Lily noticed that, as night fell, the female stopped making trips before the male did. (We spent several evenings in the classroom collecting additional data during the busiest feeding period.) This observation intrigued her, so she created a theory which connected the information from her graph to another concern the class had studied. The class had learned that some species, such as starlings and house sparrows, attack baby bluebirds and sometimes the female. This information horrified the children, and they often pointed to starlings in the school yard and worried aloud that these birds might be coming dangerously close to the bluebird family. When they saw the female hesitate before leaving the box, students theorized, "She's probably looking for predators." It made sense to Lily that her data could be explained by the female hiding from the sparrows, but she could not understand the *why* of the sparrow's behavior. Why would anything want to harm something as beautiful as a bluebird? To fill in this unresolved mystery, Lily created a mythical explanation, and by doing so, she gave us a deeper respect for the role of fiction in science.

This inclination to explain natural occurrences has captured the imagination of cultures throughout history. There were stories about how life began. There is the "fictitious" story of the ancient Egyptians who believed that frogs and toads arose from silt deposited by the flooding Nile. Charles Darwin's biological explanation, which many consider to be a much more plausible, "factual" scenario, has strong similarity to the Egyptians' story. He suggested that life arose from a small warm pond, where a rich mix of organic chemicals gave rise to the first organisms. The silt of the Nile was really not much different than the small warm pond— both describe places that have rich ingredients to generate life. We need to respect all stories. One crosses the line between fact and fiction unknowingly; the lines are blurred, but the stories are clear and honest explanations for describing our world.

Experts in the field of writing show the importance of writing about what one knows well, and understanding the relationship between writing and reading (Graves, 1983). The class's use of fiction demonstrated both of these features. All of our interest in birds influenced the way the children and teachers read stories. Whenever any bird was mentioned in a read-aloud book, the children's eyes lit up, and they talked about the species mentioned and the setting of the story. The class respected the research that fiction writers did. Sometimes the students recognized information from their own experiences, and at other times they checked details, such as the size of a nest or wing span, with a field guide or nonfiction resource. The class learned to appreciate imagery and poetic language in nonfiction sources. We adults changed as readers as well. We read *The Trumpet of the Swan* with fresh eyes and with renewed respect for the author. Writing provided the class (and adults) the opportunity to live the process that we all had appreciated as readers.

Like E. B. White, these younger authors began with what they knew. As authors write about what they know, they fill in the spaces of unanswered questions with writing about what they wish or what they imagine. In fiction people call this imagination "exaggeration;" in nonfiction they call it "theory." The edges between fact and fiction blur in the process of wondering about the mysteries of the natural world and creating stories to explain them.

Developing Skills in Using Resources

Every teacher wants students to become proficient, independent users of resources. Some of the skills that are key in this process are: consulting multiple resources; understanding the format and function of resource materials, such as the index; using reading strategies such as skimming; understanding the author's and illustrator's purpose; classifying topics in flexible ways in order to locate sources. Through this long-term study, we gained a new perspective on ways to help learners develop these skills. Most of the lessons began with students' observations or with the problems that they encountered. Multiple experiences have led us to be more aware of capitalizing upon an opportunity to highlight a strategy or skill in context, to reflect on our role as teachers, and to set goals for helping learners in the future.

Soon after the class began to use field guides, Nicholas and Scott made an important discovery. They had both seen a new species visiting the feeder. Scott found the bird in the field guide he had loaned to the class, while Nicholas located it in our class guide. When the two read aloud the narratives to each other, they found that each source gave complementary information. Scott remarked, "Maybe we should use both [books]." We asked the boys to share their discovery and their advice with the class. This experience paved the way to compare features found in multiple field guides. Some guides showed both male and female of a given species. Others included arrows pointing to key features for identification or silhouettes of selected birds in flight. The class found a wide variety of range map displays, many with specialized information. Scott's guide, for example, had color-coded maps that indicated summer, winter, and all-year ranges. These maps were easier to read than the black-and-white maps in the class guide. Other resources showed different layers of information, such as ranges for breeding and migratory routes, as well as symbols for the specialized habitats of wetlands, pine forests, or desert. Highlighting the usefulness of these different features became an important part of book-sharing time. The wide variety of books not only encouraged the children as readers, but also as writers, by showing them a wealth of options for creating their own texts. As we looked back on these experiences, we wondered how we might have raised the children's awareness of the benefits of multiple resources without Nicholas's and Scott's lead. We decided that one strategy in the future might be to encourage the children to examine a text set (including fiction and poetry) and discuss the features that they noticed in different sources. We were beginning to believe, however, that the opportunity would arise naturally if we listened closely.

Consulting a Range of Resources

Over time both children and adults brought a wide range of resources to school. Our never-ending spiral of questions led us to seek more complex and specialized sources. For example, in the spring the children observed birds nesting both at home and at school, and we discovered a specialized field guide for nests (Harrison, 1975). These specialized sources helped the children develop an awareness of the wide range of resources for a broad topic like birds. Through encountering more complex books, magazines, and newsletters, they began to develop flexible strategies for reading. Many of the more complex sources, such as the nest guide and a newsletter from Cornell Laboratory of Ornithology, were geared for an adult audience. Sometimes we would read passages from adult material to the children and discuss the ideas before offering it to the children for reading. The students helped each other the same way when they brought materials to share with the class. The children rarely complained about material being too difficult; instead they learned to scan or skim in order to find information that was meaningful or interesting to them. Reading strategies arose from a real need and desire to know.

Through other experiences, students developed an appreciation for nonprint sources other than maps, such as drawings and photographs. When we read the picture book, *Cactus Hotel* (1991), Rett commented that on every page "There is something in the pictures that's not in the writing." He pointed to one page that showed a white-winged dove's eggs, while the bird was mentioned on another page. His insight led him to study illustrations with increased appreciation. Other children spent hours studying pictures and sketching. Amanda realized that drawing was a research skill when she wrote, "What surprised me was that I would be able to take what I know and draw it."

Shunta learned that pictures, like written text, reflect an author's purpose. In the spring many students became interested in the dimensions, colors, and patterns of different species' eggs. Most of them used exact measurements as they sketched life-size eggs. Phyllis noticed that Shunta was drawing a cardinal's egg that was the size of a hen's egg. "See this egg," Shunta remarked. "I've drawn it close-up so you can see it better." She reached for a book from the class library and flipped to a page that showed an illustration of a cardinal with an enlarged version of its egg. Shunta realized that for the purpose of showing detail, a close-up rendering was useful. This appreciation for purpose influenced her a few weeks later when the class was trying to identify a nest that a fifth grader had brought to school. Shunta, referring to a photograph in the field guide of nests, instructed the class to look at the shape of the nest in the picture, but not to compare its size to the actual nest. She explained, "This picture is taken far away." Observation, experimentation, and multiple experiences helped Shunta be a strategic reader of nonprint materials.

Understanding the Format of Nonfiction Books

Often the students learned the function of other features of resources through purposeful use. Although we conducted a few planned minilessons on ways to read nonfiction, such as how to skim the table of contents, read sections in any order, skip unneeded subheadings when looking for specific topics, and so on, the best lessons occurred when a need arose in a specific context for a particular child. For example, when Mr. Kelly visited he referred to a buff-breasted sandpiper that he had spotted out of its range. Chris, intrigued by the story, wanted to know more about the bird. He knew to look in the index, but he could find no reference under *b*. He described his problem to David, who asked, "What could you look under next?" Chris decided *sandpiper*, and sure enough, he found a long list of sandpipers under that heading. He then used his new insight about the classification scheme of an index to assist him in locating a Harris's sparrow by looking under the more generic term of *sparrow*.

The children also learned about classification in an ongoing, informal way, and we believed this learning was another outcome of a long-term study. Scott was the first student to bring a field guide to school, and over the next few weeks children sought his help in locating species and interpreting range maps. Later, many students received guides for presents or borrowed them from parents and grandparents. Before long we noticed that whenever we mentioned a species in conversation or in a read-aloud book, students reached in their desks, opened to the appropriate page, and held the book in the air for classmates to see. Guest speakers never failed to mention how impressed they were with this facility in locating information. We realized that the students had taught themselves or each other. Earlier many of them had pored over pictures in a more general way, but the exploratory time, alone or with peers, afforded them the opportunity to learn how various resources were organized. Thus we learned that time is a valuable asset in helping learners be competent users of source materials.

Collaboration in Research

Interest projects provided another opportunity for the children to appreciate the role of collaboration in being a skilled researcher. In the fall the class brainstormed topics of interest based on our first weeks of observation. For example, Nikki wanted to investigate birds that feed on the ground, and Jonathan was interested in learning more about "birds that swoop." Most of the resource books that we borrowed from the library reflected general topics, such as flight or attracting birds to a feeder. Although pertinent information was often embedded in these larger topics, it was often difficult to find. We devised a strategy to address the problem of locating information by asking everyone to complete a project proposal form. Phyllis then responded with suggestions of possible resources, including interviews, titles of books, and classmates who were known to have expertise on the topic. We next constructed a large poster, listing topics such as "eating habits," "flight," and "bird behavior." Below each broad topic we wrote the names of students whose more narrow focus could be classified within a particular heading. We encouraged the children to keep an eye open for information that might be useful for their classmates, and during work times we referred children to each other. For example, Jonathan told us one day that he didn't know how to look up about birds that swoop to the feeder. Phyllis gave him a book on flight, but he wasn't satisfied. Meanwhile, Eric was studying an Audubon guide that described bird behavior. He enthusiastically described to Phyllis what he had learned about a hawk's flight. Phyllis called Jonathan over, suggested that he investigate a broader range of birds that swoop, and then invited Eric to share his newly acquired knowledge of the topic. The two boys worked together for the remainder of the period and then shared with the group descriptions of how sea birds swoop as they dive and how birds of prey position their feet. We emphasized how Eric had inadvertently found information for Jonathan as he pursued his own topic. In the days that followed many children followed Eric and Jonathan's lead, pointing out information for classmates as they read. In this way the children became more proficient at reading with specific audiences in mind: themselves as well as fellow researchers. At the same time they learned that information for one topic might be classified under several other headings. Jonathan found information about his topic from several sources: bird behavior books, references about flight, field guides, and his own observation at the window. In order to highlight the contributions of these varied sources for their projects, the children were required to record as references not only books (as in a typical bibliography), but also human resources and observations. Community support enabled the children to persist in locating information from a variety of sources. (See Appendixes B, C, and D for guides used in developing and evaluating this project.)

A Final Reflection

When we reflected on the children's growth as flexible and strategic users of resources, we saw a parallel with lessons learned from the writing process movement regarding conventions (Calkins, 1994). Opportunities to teach children strategies, whether it be quotation marks or locating a species in an index, arise naturally in the context of reading and writing. During a long-term study a range of needs can be addressed as children pursue a variety of individual questions. The experiences with bird research helped us open our eyes and ears and recognize these opportunities in the future.

Like naturalist Rudy Mancke, a sense of wonder drove the children to consult additional resources. However, at first when the children found these resources, they often summarized or copied direct passages from a book or encyclopedia. Over time, as they continued to make more direct observations about birds and pose additional theories to explain what they were seeing, they developed a broader view of what research really is. It was this cycle of observing, wondering, and consulting resources, along with collaborative discussions of their findings, that helped them become more critical consumers of these texts. They learned *not* to accept facts as unquestioned truths; they developed a persistent skepticism toward any source, whether it be an anomaly within a text, such as Shawn's questioning about a blue jay being a helpful bully, or a comparative analysis of two sources, such as Billy's decision to ask the same question of two guest speakers. They learned that knowledge changes—as it did with the range of the house finch—and that theories are tentative best guesses. They developed a broader understanding of what constitutes a resource: packages; pictures; maps; written records of friends; peers, and older experts; poetry; and fiction. Most importantly, they realized that increased knowledge leads to new questions, and that there will always be spaces in their understanding that only their imaginations can fill.

3

Inquiry Invites Exploratory Conversations

C onversations nurtured us as a community. In Chapter 1 we looked at the important conditions for supporting productive conversations. In this chapter we want to look at conversations over time, examine how the class developed certain norms for conversing, and see how together we came to appreciate the benefits of generating many theories about our observations and readings. The role of conversations is an extremely important dimension of a scientific community. In this chapter we emphasize that conversations provide a public forum for offering multiple interpretations and theories, raising new questions, revising and exploring one's own thinking, taking risks, generating hypotheses, sharing individual experiences and background knowledge, and building a sense of community. To show the diversity of conversations that occurred throughout the year we have described conversations that revolved around video observations, books, and an artifact (an unidentified bird's nest). We have also included a strategy that we called "Wonder Sheets" as an avenue for extending important issues raised in previous conversations.

Discussing a Finch Feather

In the spring several children noticed at the feeder a house finch with a feather sticking out from its back. We videotaped the event so that we could share the unique observation with the rest of the class. After sharing the tape we asked the children to interpret what they saw. This experience particularly demonstrated the role of conversation in generating multiple theories to interpret an event. Rett said that perhaps the wind pushed the feather into that position. Danielle related the awkward position of the feather to her own experience with a pet bird. "My bird does the same thing. 'Cause when we let her out of the cage, she starts to flutter around, and she starts to go all the way in a circle. Then the feathers start to stick out like that . . ." Shannon theorized, "Maybe it got in a fight with another bird, and like a feather flew off that bird." Eric offered another explanation: "Maybe before you saw him, he went to the birdbath and got his feathers wet a little bit, and he started to flap his wings. [The feather] started to stick out like after I take a bath, I brush my hair and it sticks up." Kevin added to this theory by relating an observation he had made earlier: "I think Eric's right, 'cause I saw that house finch, I think Andrew and me both saw it, and it went to the birdbath . . . and after that he did get a little in the water. I think that his feather did get wet." Thus Eric's theory prompted Kevin to share this earlier experience and to rethink its significance. Chris entered the conversation by offering some theories of his own: "I got two theories. It might have been a feather that was going to fall off of him, but he went to the birdbath, and it got stuck to him. And another one, he might have gotten in the birdbath, and there was a feather floating around, and it got stuck to his back." Chris built off the birdbath event to pose some additional explanations. In this way one theory becomes the catalyst for generating further theories. Chris was also willing to propose two theories. As a class of scientists we were learning the value of multiple theories.

Rhiannon offered still another explanation: "I thought maybe it and another house finch were showing off, and its feather got stuck like that." Billy extended this idea by saying, "Maybe he was itching, and maybe when he was itching his back, it popped the feather up." Both Rhiannon and Billy drew upon previous knowledge the class had developed about birds. We had all witnessed the male bluebird preening himself as a way to show off to the female. We had also learned that while preening, birds itch themselves to get rid of mites.

Thus the current problem of the stuck feather was an opportunity for these two children to connect these earlier insights to a new situation. In fact, regular opportunities to converse about new observations encourage this important connection making. Danielle compared the feather problem to the behavior of her own pet birds, and Eric connected the problem to his own hairbrushing experience. There was a wide range of connections, and the open-ended nature of the conversation ("Who has an explanation for what we just saw?") supported these personal ties.

Building Theories

Another important feature of this conversation is that children built off each other's ideas and were willing to offer a variety of theories. Offering theories to explain strange phenomena is risky business. We had worked hard to establish an environment that respected multiple interpretations. Learners always grow as risk takers when they know that their first ideas are not their final ideas. Rett appeared to abandon his hypothesis about the wind when he suggested his theory about fighting or hitting something. When learners know that exploratory discussions are no more than public forums for rough-draft thinking and that they will be allowed to revise their thinking at any point along the way, they grow as risk takers. Another indicator of this risk-taking stance is the kind of words that the children used to frame their thinking, such as "Maybe . . ." or "It might have . . ." By couching their theories in this tentative language, learners are telling the group that these ideas are only being considered. Even though we never found out the real cause for that rearranged feather, we still benefited from the discussion. It provided the children the opportunity to make further connections with previous knowledge and experiences, to engage in risk taking and theory building, and to participate in another generative conversation that helped define us as a collaborative community.

Living with multiple theories is a natural part of a scientific life. A parallel story from the larger scientific community emphasizes this same point. Paleontologists have struggled to answer one of the fundamental questions of human evolution: When did the first apelike creatures begin to walk upright? According to one theory, when the climate of Africa changed from moist forests to drier grasslands, hominids stood upright to spot predators lurking in the tall grasses (Gorman & Major, 1995). Other scientists argued that an upright position prevented the animal from absorbing too much heat from the tropical sun. Still others believed that walking on two feet allowed early hominids the new opportunity to use their hands to carry children, food, and other supplies. Although a new fossil discovery in Kenya is causing some paleontologists to question these theories, it is important to note that scientists entertained these multiple theories for many years. As fellow scientists in their own collaborative community, children too must be encouraged to generate various theories to explain a given phenomenon.

The Benefits of Generating Many Theories

As we reflected on the nature of the conversations that had occurred throughout the year we noticed that the class was often involved in generating multiple theories to explain particular events. We asked the children what benefits they saw in raising various theories and then later categorized their responses under these two general benefits:

1. Building many theories is a generative experience. Ashley remarked, "It's good to have a lot of theories because it raises more questions and then we get deeper into the subject. And then we get more questions and more theories, and so on." Ashley eloquently expressed the generative nature of inquiry learning. Theories don't answer questions but rather provide a basis for posing further questions. Inquiry is a process of digging deeper; it is an ever enlarging spiral that continues outward in new and unanticipated directions. For instance, when we noticed that

the female bluebird spent more time on the wire before she entered the box with food for her babies, we ventured several theories about this behavior: She was looking for potential predators; she wanted to be outdoors more because she had spent a lot of time in the box incubating the eggs; she was tired and wanted the male to help out more at this time; she was sunbathing and was trying to stay healthy; she was just more cautious than the male, and so on. These theories raised new questions, such as, "Are there any predators around? Who are they and how might they harm the bluebirds? How much will the male help in feeding the young? Is sunbathing an activity that birds really need to do?" and so on. These questions prompted us to read more and to look more closely out the window and consequently pose some additional theories. For instance, we looked more closely at the starlings and noticed that they often perched on top of a nearby light post. We wondered, "Are they watching the bluebirds and waiting for an appropriate time to attack? Are they waiting for the young to leave the nest before they attack? Are they trying to show the bluebirds that they own the territory?" and so forth. This is the never-ending trail of inquisitiveness that captures the spirit of inquiry learning.

Other children commented about this generative potential in another way. Eric remarked, "I think it's neat to have a lot of theories because other people will get more ideas. If there are a lot of theories other people can build on that, but if you have only one theory then you wouldn't have a lot of ideas." Danielle commented about the challenge of considering many ideas: "If you were stuck with just one theory you wouldn't get anywhere. If you have a lot of theories it helps you get more interested; it helps you learn more. If you have one theory you're stuck with that one thing, and you're learning just one thing." All of these children really underscored the aesthetic dimension of theory building.

Theories are aesthetic creations that learners can revise and reshape in different ways to explain new phenomena. This spirit of playfulness is a crucial, yet often neglected, part of what it means to live the life of a scientist. Danielle was attracted to the intellectual opportunity to sort, sift, and analyze different theories. She argued that settling on just one theory makes for some uninteresting conversations. Instead, what she relished was the very opposite of what textbooks present to students, where there are single-theory explanations to complex issues. She liked to think, and building theories was an intellectual task that she found challenging.

2. Building many theories helps us remain flexible thinkers. Chris addressed this issue when he commented, "If you have only one theory it could be wrong. Say we said that the female was protecting the territory—that's why she stayed on the wire longer. And then we saw the male chase away the other birds, like we saw. If we had a bunch of theories we might have the right one. But if we have only one theory we would have done all this work for nothing. If we have a lot of theories we'll probably have the right theory. If we have only one theory, then if somebody said something and didn't really think about it, and then we'd be focusing

on something that didn't even make sense, or was just plain wrong. If you go off in the direction that she is protecting the territory, and then you see the male chase away the other birds, then we'd have to change our theory and throw away all that stuff that we did." Billy agreed with Chris, "If we have a lot of ideas, one of them might be right. Like Chris said, if you only have one theory you might be focusing in the wrong direction."

Both Chris and Billy underscore the "boon and the bane of observation" (Eisner, 1991, p. 98). Knowing what to look for (through theories) makes the search more efficient. At the same time, knowing what to look for can make learners *less* likely to see things that were not a part of their expectations. Relying on just one theory is too limiting; it causes a premature focus on the problem at hand and needlessly converges thoughts and ideas.

On the other hand, multiple theories have the potential to widen the vision of how learners interpret the world. Einstein once said, "It is the theory that decides what we can observe" (John-Steiner, 1985, p.195). Eisner reiterates this same point: "Yet labels and theories are not without their costs . . . Labels and theories provide a way of seeing. But a way of seeing is also a way of not seeing. There are stock responses, and there are also stock perceptions." The children recognized the limits of having only one theory to view the world; they knew that multiple theories enabled them to remain more flexible thinkers, as they interpreted events from many different perspectives. In summary, whether the children were constructing theories about happenings long ago, such as the mysterious appearance of the cattle egret (Chapter 2), or current observations, such as the ruffled feather on a finch, it did not matter. What did matter was that they were actively engaged in the business of building, abandoning, and revising theories. In short, they were learning what it means to live the life of a naturalist.

Discussing the Rise and Fall of Bluebirds

Conversations also provide learners a public forum for making personal connections with new topics and current observations. One strategy for promoting these connections is to invite children to respond to nonfiction texts (as discussed earlier in Chapter 2). There are stories in nonfiction texts, just as much as they are in works of fiction. Harold Rosen has remarked, "What is geology but a vast story that geologists have been composing and revising throughout the existence of their subject? Indeed what has the recent brouhaha about evolution been but two stories competing for the right to be the authorized version, the authentic story . . . There are stories wherever we turn . . ." (Rosen, 1985, p.16). We encouraged the children to be active storytellers as they listened and responded to nonfiction texts. During our bluebird investigation we, as teachers, became interested in the history of the bluebird in this country. As we shared the story aloud, children contributed their own stories, thereby enriching the collective story of our scientific community.

A Short History of the Eastern Bluebird

As the female bluebird began to build her nest outside our window, we read all that we could about the Eastern bluebird. David became especially interested in the history of the bluebird and wanted to share this recently acquired information with the class. He was particularly intrigued with their history because neither he nor Phyllis had seen bluebirds when they were younger. The text he was reading helped to explain why this was so. He shared with the children that people actually put up nest boxes for bluebirds in the 1800s (Stokes, D. & Stokes, L., 1991, p.16). It is believed that the bluebirds were quite common in the 1700s and 1800s because of the extensive cutting of forests, the planting of apple orchards, and the use of fence posts. It is believed that the beginning of the decline of the Eastern bluebird occurred when two foreign species of birds were introduced into this country: the house sparrow in 1850 and the starling in 1890. Both of these European birds are very aggressive and compete with the bluebird for nesting cavities. The house sparrow will enter a bluebird box, kill the female, and remove any eggs that might be there. Within fifty years the population of these two birds exploded so dramatically that by 1900 the house sparrow was the most common bird in North America and by 1940 the starling had spread to almost every part of the United States and southern Canada. However, the continual development of nest box trails, beginning in the 1970s, has helped to reverse the decline in the bluebird population.

Collaborative Exploratory Conversations

After sharing this part of the bluebird story with the children, David asked, "Why do you suppose open farmland, apple orchards, and fence posts were helpful to bluebirds? Let's talk about that together. At the end of our conversation I am going to expect everyone to write a reflection on what they found interesting about our talk, and what they are now wondering about. Be thinking about these questions as we have our conversation." We found it helpful to let children know ahead of time that they would be expected to write this reflection so they could be listening for ideas that they might wish to elaborate on later. These reflections demonstrate to children that conversations are an important part of classroom life; they also force each person to lay claim to her own insights and connections.

Although the text did mention a few reasons that seemed to answer David's question about apple orchards and fence posts, he chose not to share those initially; instead he wanted the children to make their own personal connection to this phenomenon. Brent started the conversation by offering several explanations for why these conditions might be favorable to bluebirds: "There are apples around and insects get on all kinds of fruits and vegetables; insects would be on the apples, and they [the bluebirds] could get them. And they like to go on to those posts, like that's what they had in one of those pictures [in a book he had read] . . . And when they cut down the forest, it gave them [the bluebirds] more room if they could swoop around and spot insects down below."

Andrew wondered if apple trees might have a lot of holes in them for nesting and then connected the discussion to some research that he had done earlier on his computer and posted on the class bulletin board: "The thing that I typed up on the computer—it says that they live in apple trees, and they live in holes in trees like woodpeckers." Phyllis added to this observation, "Yes, they live in holes that woodpeckers make. Bluebirds cannot make their own cavities. They have to live in somebody else's cavity." Andrew's comment helped the class recognize a similarity between these two species. Since Phyllis and David were well-acquainted with apple orchards from living in New England, Phyllis added some details about the characteristics of this kind of tree: "The branches are all twisty, and there's little places where the branches twist up near one another, and they make nice little holes. So apple trees sort of have natural holes." Phyllis naturally shared her past experience because she was comfortable in this community and she was responding to Andrew's question about apple trees having holes. We have found that children and adults can be co-equals in classroom conversations because, despite the difference in age, they both have experience in the world, and so both can contribute "mutually valued resources" (Woodward & Serebrin, 1989).

As the discussion continued other children offered additional personal connections. Rett suggested, "Well, I was thinking it helped the bluebirds a lot because people built farms, and bluebirds like open fields. And they put those apple trees—I read in a book that bluebirds like apple halves, you know, so they would like to eat the apples. And the fences—I believe I heard that bluebirds like to be right up on fences, so they can see like all around, and they can see if there are predators around. And that helps them a lot." We had all noticed that our own bluebirds liked to perch on the wire and look around the courtyard. Rett was using this current observation to make sense of this story of the bluebird's past. Like Brent and Andrew, he also connected the discussion to a book he had read earlier and then raised a new issue about predation.

Ashley picked up on this idea: "Since Rett went on about predators, my grandma tells me that bluebirds, well, and other birds, like to perch on fences, and I think it's good for bluebirds . . . cause if they didn't burn all the land down [i.e., clear the land for farming], the predators would be coming around and they [the bluebirds] wouldn't be able to build their nest." Rett's concern for predators provided a bridge for Ashley to tie together information from her grandmother and her current theory about why clearing the land was beneficial for bluebirds. Ashley also began her commentary by acknowledging the source of her ideas, "Since Rett went on about predators . . ." We tried to encourage this mutual recognition of ideas throughout the year. When we saw one child building off the idea of another, we would make that act public by saying, for instance, "Ashley, I noticed that you took Rett's idea of predators and used it to talk about your own theory." We wanted children to appreciate the value of a community in helping us all make our own personal connections, and to realize that what we come to know together is far greater than what any of us could have done alone. Acknowledging the source of our own thinking is one strategy for celebrating this collaborative potential.

William continued the conversation: "Well, it's like a theory and a comment put together. Because if there were a lot of apple trees and a lot of room, more of them could move in at one time. Because if, like, you said apple trees had holes in them? (David nodded his head). They could provide homes for them . . . (David nodded his head again). And also there's a lot of room for them. (David then paused to speak to two children who were whispering to each other, thereby giving William some additional time to organize his thoughts.) If there is a lot of room and a lot of apple trees, and the apple trees have holes in them, that could provide homes for them, so more of them could move in at one time." At first, William used David to check his understanding of a couple of points; then, after a brief interruption in the conversation, he was able to summarize his main thoughts. His last thoughts seemed the most polished and tied his points together in the most succinct fashion. However, it was the nature of the conversation that allowed this kind of exploration. Talk has a fluid, dynamic quality that gives learners the opportunity to exchange and revise ideas with peers rather quickly. Scientific conversations must capitalize on this tentative, exploratory nature of talk.

Children Reflect About the Birds

As the children wrote reflections on this conversation about the history of bluebirds, they commented on several major issues. One of the most disturbing parts of the discussion was the adversarial relationship between the bluebirds and the starlings and house sparrows. Nikki wondered, "I wonder why the starling goes after the bluebird." Rett compared the two predators by examining their range maps and then predicted which one would be the most harmful to the bluebirds: "I think that the house sparrows have a better chance of reducing the (bluebird) population because I looked in one of my bird books and the house sparrow covers a little bit more of Canada than the starling." Thus, Rett extended the conversation by consulting additional resources and then making a further prediction (although his comparison is slightly misleading because his range map did not reflect density, an issue that we had discussed occasionally throughout the year). William hypothesized about the other long-term effects of the presence of these two predators on the bluebirds: "The house sparrow and starling might have made the bluebirds even dislike their friends." Ashley used this current information about starlings to interpret some of the observations the class had been making about starlings they had sighted around the portable: "I think that the starlings are looking over the bluebirds and just waiting a little while until there is no other bird around, and (then) they would probably attack the bluebirds and peck them to death, which would be very unpleasing to see." The discussion enabled her to view the present classroom circumstances with new eyes. Several children commented about the dangers of introducing a non-native species into a new habitat. Shunta wrote: "I think they shouldn't put other birds in different state(s) because it is very dan- ger(ous) and now a lot of birds are (going to) die. I wonder: If we take them back to Europe when we catch them, will they kill those birds too (i.e., other birds in Europe)?" Shunta also extended the class discussion in a new way by wondering about the effects of trying to reverse the introduction of starlings. If such a reversal were even possible, would starlings be hostile to other birds or do they have a par- ticular hostility toward bluebirds?

Another facet of the conversation that intrigued several students was the eco- logical interdependence of apple trees, insects, and bluebirds. Jonathan wrote: "I think that the reason they put out apple orchards is that apples bring insects, like beetles and worms, and bluebirds feed their young insects. I think the fences help bluebirds (because) they can fly on to that (fence post) and then they can go into the bluebird box more better because they perched on something to get their bal- ance." Chris wrote about this same interdependence: "I think when the fence posts were built maybe plants with berries twined around it like ivy. Then after the post rotted a lot of bugs came. I also think apple orchards attracted bugs. I also think apple orchards made hole homes" (Figure 3-1).

Other children wondered about the present situation of our own bluebirds. Andrew personalized the issue of predation and analyzed a current situation that he had observed by connecting it to this problem with predators: "The bluebirds are very protective of the nest and the area, and when two chickadees were around the box the male (bluebird) dive-bombed the two chickadees." The issue of preda- tors was on Billy's mind when he wondered about the nest-building behavior of the bluebirds: "I wonder if bluebirds will nest in the branches where they have like already built a nest. Would bluebirds use any part of the apple (tree) for the nest?" We had seen an empty nest in the crab apple tree outside the window and Billy hypothesized that it belonged to the bluebird because of all the discussion about apple orchards.

Thus, this exploratory conversation and reflection time allowed each one of us to share our personal connections with bluebirds and contribute to the common knowledge base. However, these collaborative discussions did not settle all the is- sues but rather served to raise new ones: How might predators affect our blue- birds? How will our bluebirds respond? What is the behavior of bluebirds toward other species? What is the behavior of starlings toward other birds, especially those birds living in England? How is it possible to control a nonindigenous species? We were all left with more questions than we came with, and that is as it should be in collaborative, exploratory conversations, even if one of the members of the con- versation is the author of a book. Children recognized this author, as well as other

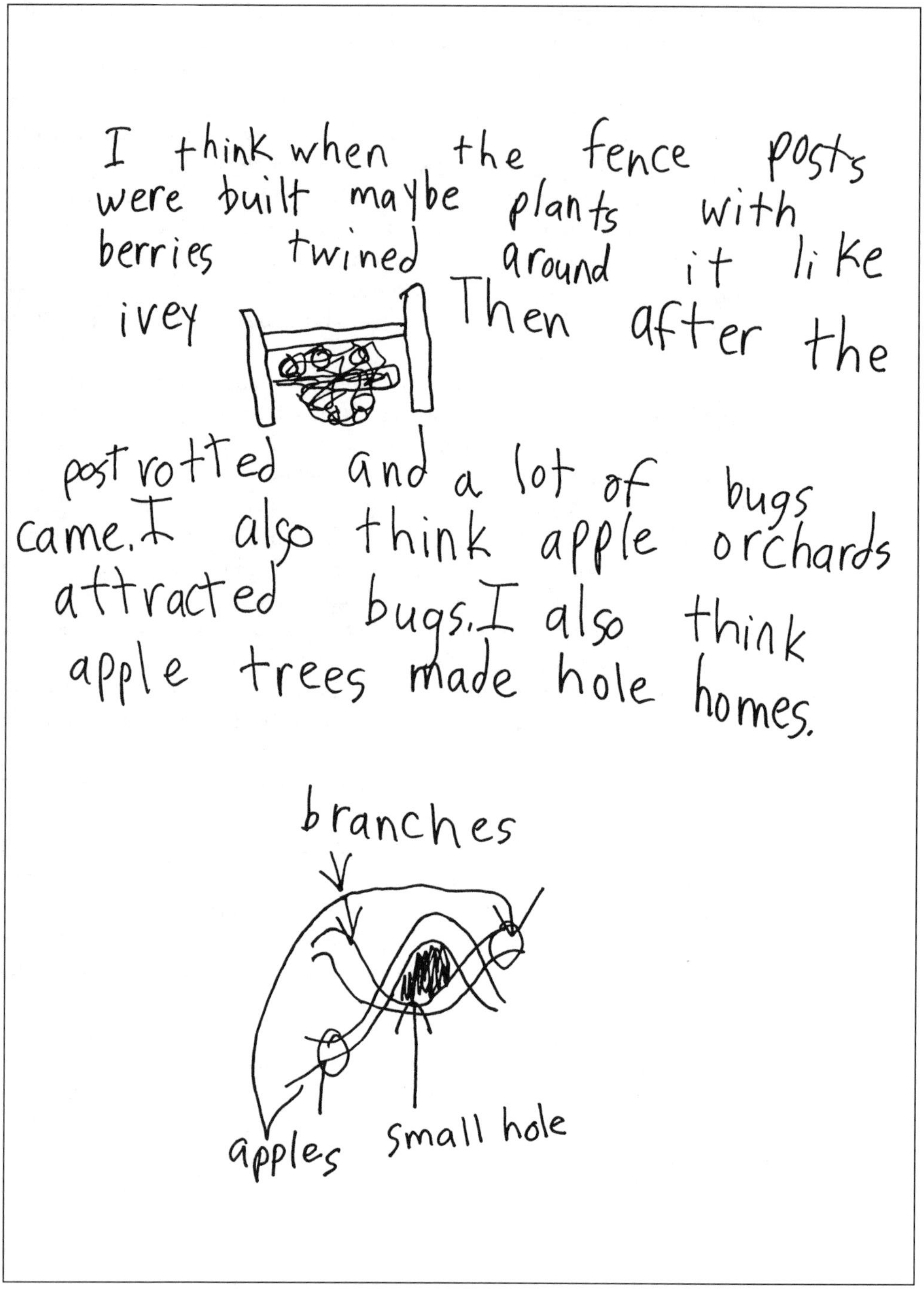

I think when the fence posts were built maybe plants with berries twined around it like ivey Then after the post rotted and a lot of bugs came. I also think apple orchards attracted bugs. I also think apple trees made hole homes.

branches

apples small hole

FIG 3–1 *Chris Interprets the History of Bluebirds*

authors, as distant mentors who could contribute to our ongoing conversations. The children used these authors as they did any other resource by comparing the current text to what they already knew, and by questioning, challenging, and extending the text in order to pose fresh hypotheses about bird behavior. Both students and teachers found themselves turning to texts because they were full of questions and current observations, and they came away with more of the same. That's the dynamic nature of reading and discussing nonfiction texts.

Teachers Reflect on Exploratory Conversations

As we reflected upon the nature of this conversation, we also realized that the children were viewing the history of bluebirds from multiple perspectives. The different stances that the children took naturally reflected the personal connections they made with the topic. They drew upon the fields of history (the rise and decline of farmland), botany (the structure of apple trees for cavities and the availability of their fruit), and two branches of zoology, ornithology (the behavior of bluebirds and the impact of starlings and house sparrows), and entomology (the availability of insects around fruit trees and open fields). This interconnectedness is expressed eloquently by the well-known naturalist John Muir: "When we try to pick out anything by itself, we find it hitched to everything else in the universe (Muir, 1911, p. 110)." When people in the scientific community lose sight of these connections, they become limited in their understanding of how the world works. A prime example comes from the field of geology. The acceptance of the theory of plate tectonics (the movement of continents) by the scientific community in the 1960s was a revolutionary event that provided a common ground for all scientists who study the earth:

> Oceanographers now know that what goes on under the earth's crust affects ocean basins, paleontologists routinely use the evidence available in fossils to track the wandering of the continents across the globe, and geophysicists understand the earth's interior as a dynamic convecting system that drives the restless crust. Scientists now see planet Earth as a single integrated whole, rather than a series of isolated systems that have nothing to do with one another. (Hazen & Trefil, 1991, p. 183)

As a classroom of fellow scientists the children experienced a parallel vision of the "integrated whole." They too used different perspectives that the fields of history, botany, and geology afforded them to expand their own theories and ask further questions. Thus, the discussion about the history of bluebirds served as a model for what happens in conversations about plate tectonics. Having an array of different perspectives for explaining an event enhances the theoretical understanding of the larger community. Dewey has argued that schools ought to be embryos of the larger society (Dewey, 1916, 1966). We would argue that classrooms ought to be embryos of the larger scientific community as well. They ought to be doing what scientific communities do, such as sharing personal knowledge and experiences, and viewing phenomena from interdisciplinary perspectives. The issues may be different, but the processes and problems are the same.

Wonder Sheets: A Strategy for Continuing the Conversation

As the children made more and more observations about the bluebirds and recorded them in our daily class journal, we felt frustrated in not having enough time for everyone to discuss the significance of these observations. Therefore, we devised a strategy which we labeled Wonder Sheets. We selected what we felt were important observations that the children had been noting consistently in the daily journal and typed them on a piece of paper for everyone to respond to. In this way everyone had the opportunity to take a stand on these observations. These were the four observations and questions that we listed during the bluebirds' nest building:

1. The male and female bluebirds seem to take turns as they go in the box. What is your theory about this behavior?

2. We usually see bluebirds only in the morning. What is your theory about this behavior?

3. We have noticed that the bluebirds perch mostly on the roof, the wire, and the top of the tree. They also seem to face the sun a lot. What is your theory about this behavior?

4. What do these observations make you wonder about?

One of the real benefits of this strategy was that the children generated a host of theories that raised fresh issues, posed new questions, and sent us all back to the window with a broader view of what to look for. These points are best illustrated by looking at the children's responses to the second question.

The children had a number of interesting explanations as they interpreted why we usually see bluebirds in the morning. First, Danny challenged the observation by writing, "This is not always true. We have been seeing them in the afternoon." Inquirers are not afraid to question the observations of others. Danny had noticed a change in the activity of the bluebirds and he wanted us to consider the reasons for that change. Jonathan, as well as several other children, suggested the noise of the students as a factor: "They probably come in the morning because they know that people are usually not out in the morning." This issue of our relationship with the bluebirds was an intriguing one that children kept referring to as the year progressed. For instance, when the young hatched and we put out meal-worms on a tray for the bluebirds to eat, we noticed that after awhile the bluebirds would not fly away as they usually did but would actually watch us from a short distance away. Here again a theory to explain one particular behavior raises an important issue for the children to follow in other situations. Nikki suggested that the heat of the day might be a factor: "Maybe the bluebirds like the cold air and not the hot air. Maybe they might get tireder in the hot sun just like me. I get tired easier in the sun. That's how I am because I get all sweaty in the sun." Cortney wrote about food: "Probably so they can get more nutrients before any other birds wakes up." Several children hypothesized about the daily schedule of birds: William wrote, "I think they like to get the work done ahead of time." Scott suggested, "Well, they could work in the morning, sleep in the afternoon, and work a little at night."

We all wondered what our bluebirds did when we did not see them and Scott argued that they might do a little more work at night when none of us were there. Danielle wrote, "Maybe they have a schedule" and Lily wondered, "Maybe because they get their work done in the morning (so) they can have a long break before the next day." Brent hypothesized that the bluebirds appeared in the morning ". . . so other birds don't see them." Thus, the issues of protection, food, weather, daily schedule, and relationship with humans were all raised by the children. Of course, these issues in turn conjured up new questions to consider: How do birds protect themselves? When and how often do birds eat? Do all birds eat at the same time? How does weather affect birds? Do birds have some predictable daily schedule that they follow? We witnessed again how questions beget questions.

Thus, the Wonder Sheets provided a written record of our conversations. They made a permanent trail of our thinking and offered a tool for curricular planning. Because the issues of eating, protection, and weather were intriguing ones for the children, we tried to frame future observations with some of these same topics in mind. Wonder Sheets were also another strategy for binding us together as a community. They became a written forum to preserve everyone's voice; these sheets were placed in the bluebird journal for everyone to read and think about further. They helped us all reflect on the most compelling aspects of our previous conversations.

Examining the Norms of Classroom Conversations

Through our conversations we not only began to recognize the benefits of generating many theories, but we also began to notice that, as a community, we developed certain norms for conversing with each other. These acted as unspoken rules that governed the way our discussions proceeded. As we looked back on the many conversations that we had over the year, we noted the following unwritten expectations:

1. Entertain multiple theories. When the children considered why the bluebirds might be more active in the morning, several of them hypothesized that food, weather, or protection might be factors. The norm implied that the more theories there were, the more potential there was for new connections and unanticipated relationships.

2. Share rough-draft thinking. It was acceptable to lay bare our current thinking, even if any of us were still in the process of trying to make sense of a particular event. Partially formed ideas were legitimate contributions to the discussion.

3. Recognize and extend the contributions of others. In this way we all made public the trail of our thinking and gave credit to the social origins of our ideas.

4. Draw upon personal knowledge to make sense of current observations. Stephanie and her love birds, Brent and his ducks, and Ashley and her grandmother were prime examples of this kind of personal interpretation.

5. Use past issues as frameworks for discussing current phenomena. For instance, the issue of predation was one that the children had explored all year. They used it in the fall to explain aggressive behavior around the feeders and they used it again in the spring to explain the male bluebird's reason for perching on a nearby wire.

6. Remain open to new explorations. There was no purpose in forcing premature closure on a discussion. Instead, we learned that trying to address one question merely raised more questions to consider. Living with new questions and unresolved issues was another important norm that we developed over time.

These norms evolved throughout the year. One way to look closely at the cumulative development of these norms is to examine a conversation that occurred near the end of the school year. It is a particularly significant conversation because it shows an uninterrupted discussion (among a small group of children) that took place, for the most part, without the teacher being present. The conversation shows how the internalized norms of a community led to their expression in a smaller group setting.

Investigating a Mystery Nest

An artifact can sometimes inspire exploratory conversations. An example of such a conversation occurred in the spring when a child from a fifth-grade class brought a nest to our class. A neighbor had given her the nest, and she was hoping that our class, which had gained a reputation for its expertise on birds, could identify the nest for her. (We had discussions with our own children about not tampering with nests without a permit. A 1973 Federal law forbids such activity. Since this present nest was already disturbed, we decided to examine it.) Phyllis left the nest out on a table during writing time and invited interested children to try to identify it. It was a small, round nest, composed mostly of grasses and sphagnum moss. It had a soft lining on the inside and even contained a strand or two of plastic Easter-type grass. It had an inside depth of 1½ inches. Brent, Billy, and Amanda chose to work on this particular task (Figure 3-2).

Billy had completed a project on clutch sizes, and Amanda had created life-size models of various eggs out of play dough she brought from home. Thus, these two children already had an interest in nests and eggs and were anxious to delve into this investigation. Phyllis left them alone for awhile and then returned later to see what they had discovered. Brent said that they had first measured the nest in inches, centimeters, and millimeters. They used the chart of nest sizes we had developed earlier (Figure 1-2) as a resource for trying to identify this mystery nest.

FIG 3–2   *Amanda, Billy and Brent Examining the Mystery Nest*

They compared their measurements to the measurements on the chart and tried to find a match (they sometimes confused centimeters, millimeters, and inches; however, with continued functional use and the support of each other, they became more proficient over time).

While they continued to work, they didn't stay with this strategy completely. As they began to share their current thinking with Phyllis, they referred to birds they were familiar with and tried to make a decision about whether or not these birds were possibilities. Their first comments to Phyllis were:

Amanda: . . . And we're thinking it's a hummingbird's egg.
Brent: It's not no hummingbird nest.
Amanda: It looks like one because hummingbirds only lay two eggs.
Brent: But the hummingbird nest is taller and down into the nest. It's wide down into the nest.
Billy: Yeah, this is wide down. 'Cause this is down as big as my pencil.
Brent: It's not very big.
Billy: Yes it is.
Amanda: I'll get my eggs so we can see how many.

A Scientific Community Inquires

There are several interesting features of this conversation. First, Amanda refused to back down when Brent challenges her initial statement that it could be a hummingbird nest. Instead, she justified her thinking by saying that it looked like two hummingbird eggs could fit inside this mystery nest. By explaining the reasons for her decision Amanda helped to continue the conversation. Second, Brent responded to her explanation by arguing that the shape of the hummingbird's nest, not its size, did not match the present nest (a hummingbird's nest is unusually tall from the upper edge of the nest to its base). Thus, Amanda's explanation enabled him to raise another attribute for the group to consider when identifying a nest. Third, the children used their own language of "wide down" to describe the depth and shape of a hummingbird nest. Conversations enable learners to frame their mathematical understandings of dimension in their own way. Fourth, when Billy and Brent disagreed about the relative size of the nest Amanda proposed a test to resolve the dispute. She had made models of the eggs of various species, and she decided to place these model eggs in the nest to see if they would fit. Conversations allow learners the opportunity to draw upon previous experiences to help resolve current issues the group is confronting.

The discussion continued as the children looked at the eggs that Amanda made and estimated whether or not they thought the eggs would make an appropriate fit.

Billy: Put two hummingbird eggs (in the nest).

Brent: Definitely not hummingbird eggs.

Amanda: Cardinal . . .

Brent: Could be a cardinal. How many eggs can it lay?

Amanda: Five. A cardinal lays . . .

Billy: It's not a cardinal.

Brent: It can lay *three* to five, so that could be it.

Billy: A cardinal would probably need a bigger nest.

Brent: How about a bluebird?

Billy: No, it's not a bluebird.

Amanda: A goldfinch.

Brent: Probably a goldfinch.

Billy: A goldfinch?

Brent: Yeah, it could be. How many can it lay?

Amanda: Four to five.

Brent: Yeah, it will. It would fit. (They call Phyllis over again to share their thinking.) We think we figured it out. We think it might be a goldfinch egg (nest).

Billy: (Looking up the clutch size in a book.) Here it is. Goldfinch. It lays four to six, commonly five. Four to five eggs. (They place the model of the goldfinch egg in the nest.)

Brent: Let's see if someone has an actual model, a three-d (dimensional) model of the bird (the goldfinch).

Amanda: I can make a three-d.

Brent: Let's make a goldfinch and see if we can put it on here (the nest) and see what it would look like.

As the conversation continued the children raised other issues. Although one of Amanda's eggs might look fine in the nest, Brent reminded the group that clutch size was another factor they had to consider. After that point in the conversation the children kept referring to the book to check the size of the clutch, and then they estimated whether or not that many eggs would fit in the nest. However, even the statistics that the book provided did not resolve all cases so quickly. When Billy argued that five cardinal eggs could not possibly fit in the nest, Brent pointed to the range of three to five and reasoned that perhaps the lower limit of three could fit. His argument then caused Billy to reflect on his explanation; Billy argued that the size of a parent cardinal would dictate a larger nest.

Conversations allow learners the opportunity to challenge the decisions of others and give the owners of certain ideas the chance to reflect on their own line of reasoning. Through the help of others, learners clarified their own thinking and were rescued from being too narrow-minded in thinking about alternative perspectives. It is also interesting to note that even when the size and the number of goldfinch eggs seemed to fit in the nest, Brent suggested that they ought to test their hypothesis further by placing a three-dimensional model in the nest to see if that seemed like a logical fit. He may have raised this issue of size partly because it was the same argument that Billy had used on him earlier in the conversation when he suggested that the size of the cardinal would not be a logical fit. Thus, sometimes conversations give learners the opportunity to hear the reasoning of others and then test out that same form of argumentation themselves. Brent may have also suggested these three-dimensional models because he was involved in a bird project himself in which he made some life-size models of birds that he placed on a large mural. Again, conversations allow learners the opportunity to draw upon their previous experiences to solve current problems.

Uncovering New Evidence

Billy turned the conversation in another direction when he began to examine the composition of the nest. He reported to the group, "I looked at it, and I found that it has Easter Bunny stuff in it (the grass). And it looks like the bird is sewing it 'cause it's going around and around." His comment immediately made a connection with Amanda who said, "Hold on. This stuff grows in a plant in people's houses." She later referred to it as "fake grass" (we believe that she was referring to sphagnum moss, a common, decorative filler for potted plants) and continued her reasoning, "What I want to know is what some of these plants are. I know this is a fake . . . My mom's . . . you know how they have those plants with the fake grass in the bottom . . . This is fake grass . . . it might be a house finch . . . cause house finches stay by the house, close to the house." Brent suggested that it also could be a house wren because it too builds nests near houses. Thus, Billy's close examination of the nest gave Amanda the opportunity to build another theory.

Billy also focused on how the nest was made, as if it was sewn together "around and around." This particular attribute intrigued him, and he returned to it later in the conversation when he began looking over again the chart of nests and sharing descriptions of how some were made. At one point he read that the nests of the starlings are "sloppily built" and he asked the group if they thought the present nest was "carefully built or sloppily built." His observation caused him to read the descriptions of the nests with a new purpose in mind, and he then shared this new language with the group.

This issue of using language to describe events in the natural world was one that we had confronted during the first week of school when the children debated the different connotations for words like *peck, bump, nudge,* and others (Chapter 1). Here they were eight months later still facing the same difficulty. Billy raised the issue of the quality of nest construction and asked his friends to consider this new attribute. Some argued the nest was sloppily built because some material hung down slightly from the bottom while others maintained that it was carefully built because of the intricate weaving. The children were really debating the question,

"How do we define a sloppily built nest? What criteria should be applied?" Struggling with these nuances of language only came about because we shared our observations in a collaborative community. Honing, refining, and questioning language is a vital part of living the life of a naturalist. In addition, Billy's concern for the language of scientists was also significant for another reason. Because the children had lived through this experience as writers, struggling to communicate their observations as they sat by the window, they could better appreciate the problem as readers. As a community they were becoming more critical readers because they had been equally critical writers and speakers.

An Ongoing Conversation

When writing time concluded these three children had made a paper goldfinch and placed it in the nest. Although they seemed quite satisfied that this species was the owner of the nest, Billy kept pushing his friends to consider other possibilities by asking, "O.K. What other small bird could fit in that nest?" They rejected the blue jay as being too large but considered the towhee as an option because of the size of the eggs and the clutch size. Billy kept refusing to close down the conversation. Just as we never found out the cause of that rumpled finch feather described earlier in this chapter, so also we never identified this mystery nest for certain. However, the children still learned a great deal from the conversation. They learned together the importance of justifying their thinking, raising alternative interpretations, proposing tests to resolve disagreements, and drawing upon past experiences to explain current issues. They were demonstrating some of the norms of conversation that were helping to define us as a scientific community.

A Final Reflection

At the end of the school year we asked the children to complete a questionnqaire on our study of birds. One of the questions included, "Our class has spent many hours talking together about our wonders and theories. How did these conversations help you learn more about birds?" These are some of the children's responses:

Amanda: The wonders and theories help me think of more wonders and that makes me want to look at books.
Andrew: [Conversations helped me] because we would build a lot of people's wonders up.
Danielle: They helped me develop more ideas, and the more the ideas, the more interested I got.
Deidre: Our conversations helped me learn more about birds by us giving a wonder and then we would keep adding to the wonder until we answered a lot of the wonders.

Cortney: It helped me when one little idea and another little idea makes a big idea.
Jenny: [Conversations helped me] because as we talked I got more ideas, so now I
know ideas help.

These comments underscore the generative nature of scientific conversations. Children noted that the sharing of numerous ideas enabled them all to go farther than any of them could have gone alone. They saw the benefits of building off of each other's ideas, such as becoming more interested in exploration, revisiting books with a renewed sense of purpose and wonder, and creating new theories by combining several ideas. Conversations were the ties that bound us together and truly legitimized us as a scientific community.

4

Inquiry Focuses and Refocuses Investigations

Inquiry explorations are always shifting. Carolyn Burke has described this quality as "focused and refocused investigations" (1995). We found that from time to time there would be a refocusing on a certain intriguing aspect of the larger study. In this chapter we will discuss two such instances: refocusing our attention on the behavior of bluebirds that established their home in our nesting box, and refocusing our attention on an ecological problem known as forest fragmentation. We did not anticipate either investigation.

In the first instance, the children were in awe of the recent bluebird activity outside the classroom window and wanted to know more; in the second instance, Phyllis raised a question about forest fragmentation that was interesting to her, and soon the whole class was looking closely at this current environmental problem. Both these experiences demonstrate how mathematics naturally enters the investigation, not because it is forced into the conversation in some artificial way, but because it rides the wake of an inquiring mind. These examples also parallel a common feature of scientific communities: New findings can shift the focus of a particular investigation. For example, an American geologist recently found in the Mexican desert what could be the world's oldest animal fossil, the outline of a jellyfishlike creature that lived on the ocean floor up to 600 million years ago (*State*, Oct. 1995). This finding has the potential to shift the search for early animal life from Australia, Russia, and Africa to the American continent. Thus, the investigations in this chapter closely reflect the shifting nature of the explorations that occur in the larger scientific community.

Sometimes a mathematical tool enabled the class to investigate an issue that captured their attention. The children used the tool of graphing to document their interest in the nesting behavior of bluebirds. However, the foundation for our use of graphing had been laid several months earlier. We found several interesting graphs in Cornell Lab's newsletter, *Birdscope*. We shared these graphs with the children in order to generate some interest in the use of this tool and also to demonstrate that graphing is a valuable way for scientists to understand bird behavior. One of the graphs that we shared was an index of the black-capped chickadee group sizes that were observed in five states and one province during the winter of 1993–1994 (Figure 4-1).

We gave each child a copy of the graph, briefly explained how the graph was set up, and then asked the children, "What do people notice about this graph?" We have found this question to be an effective one to pose because it is broad enough for children to describe the data in multiple ways. Some children gave metaphorical descriptions of the shape of the data: Rhiannon wrote that "NJ looks like the Texas plains. ME looks like a trail with a lot of hills and a few holes and drops." Chris described NY as a "mountain" and the shape of the middle four lines as "a wild roller coaster." Andrew wrote that the "dots look like bunches of birds on power lines in the distance and the flying V flying high over head (referring to the top line for ME)." He also noted that the lines reminded him of a "wake when you go real fast on a boat" while William compared them to "damaged or bent railroad tracks." The children interpreted the graph in different ways as well: Danielle wrote, "I saw that the lower (the more southern) the states get the fewer amount of birds [are] seen in a flock." Chris noted, "When it's colder there's more

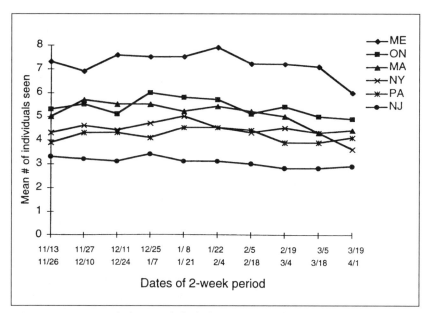

FIG 4–1   *Variation in Black-Capped Chickadee Group Size (from* Birdscope, *Cornell Laboratory of Ornithology, reprinted with permission)*

chickadees. It gets less and less chickadees in the flocks as it [the lines] goes down." William offered a theory to explain the data: "Since it's colder in the North I think birds fly in flocks more because they give off body heat to each other and that keeps them warm." Amanda added a question: "I have a wonder. In Maine they have more birds [in a flock] when it's colder. How come when it's cold down here we don't have a lot of birds [in large flocks]?" Chris answered Amanda's query by pointing out the limited focus of the data, "This [graph] doesn't tell the whole year so it might not be that many chickadees in the whole year."

As we look back on this sharing of data from the Cornell Lab we realized that several important demonstrations were being made: (1) graphs are a valuable way to show relationships, interpret bird behavior, and hypothesize about the reasons for these relationships; (2) graphs are limited in what they can convey, and learners need to be skeptical of any graphic display; (3) the shape of data can be described in metaphorical terms (Many children were intrigued with the different symbols for each state and later on invented some of their own symbols to designate important aspects of their own investigations.); and (4) probably the biggest demonstration of all was that graphs were a useful tool for scientists. In fact, the data that we shared was obtained from the Lab's annual Project FeederWatch, the largest scientific experiment in the country. Thousands of people (almost all amateurs) across the country send in data about birds that they have observed in their particular area. Cornell tabulates the results and publishes them in their newsletter. We stressed to the class that amateurs have made important contributions to our understanding of bird behavior; we were validating children as scientists in their own right by inviting them to examine data from the larger scientific community. In fact, amateurs continue to make contributions in all areas of science. It was an amateur astronomer who made the recent discovery of a comet slamming into Jupiter; another amateur discovered the famous prehistoric "ice man" that lay buried in the Alps for thousands of years. Amateurs play an important role in advancing our understanding of the world. The children were coming to appreciate this valuable perspective.

Collecting Data to Understand the Behavior of Bluebirds

This discussion about the Cornell graphs provided a useful demonstration for us as we started to collect our own data. We found ourselves refocusing our attention on the bluebirds when we first saw the female one morning with some pine straw (pine needles) in her beak. She kept making numerous trips to the box and the children were amazed that she was working so hard. It was this awe at her persistence in nest building that caused us to begin to count the number of times she was coming and going, as well as the amount of time she was gone. David set up a chart to begin to record this data, and the children used the classroom clock and a few of their own stopwatches to do the timing. It is important to note here that it was the wonder that came first; we then used the mathematical concepts of time and quantity (number of trips) to help us frame our question in another way. The mathematics arose naturally as a meaningful tool to address the questions and satisfy the wonders that learners hold about their world. The data that we began to collect about bluebirds was certainly an example of how mathematics not only helped the class in understanding the behavior of these birds but also enabled us to build new theories and raise fresh questions.

After gathering data about the bluebirds for several days, we invited a few children to make a graph to show the data in another way. We found that working with a small group of students first was a helpful strategy; they provided still another demonstration of what's possible for the rest of the classroom community. Danielle worked on one of these early graphs (Figure 4-2) and Deidre and Nikki worked together on the other one (Figure 4-3). Both graphs show how the same set of data can be displayed in different ways. Danielle's graph indicated the chronology of events by documenting the exact sequence of the female's trips. We wondered why some of these longer times occurred during the middle of the day. Deidre and Nikki showed the most frequently occurring times by categorizing the times into four periods: thirty seconds, one minute, two minutes, and more than two minutes. This graph indicated that the thirty-second and the one-minute trips

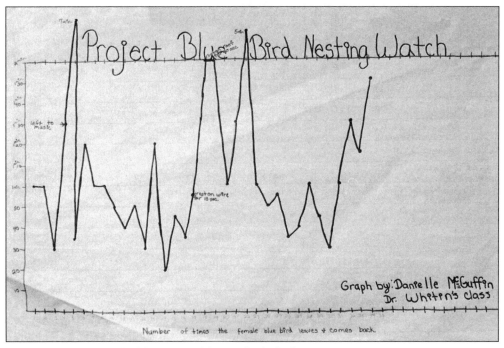

FIG 4–2   *Danielle's Graph of the Nesting of the Female Bluebird*

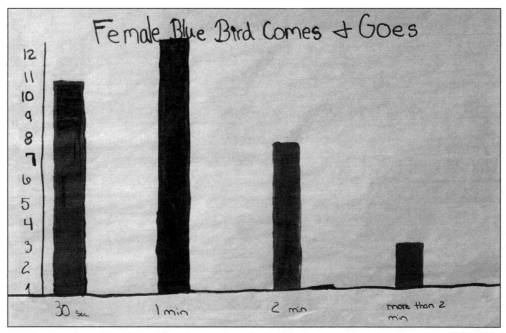

FIG 4–3   *Deidre and Nikki's Graph of the Nesting of the Female Bluebird*

were the most frequent and we wondered how long the female could keep up that pace. Jenny commented about the difference between these two graphs by noting, "The bar graph showed how many times it was and the line graph showed all the ups and downs." Thus, each graph provided a unique visual display that offered new insights and raised further questions about the nesting behavior of the female bluebird.

These girls also shared with the class some problems they encountered as they constructed the graphs. We had asked them to create a title for their graphs but the children were not sure what to call them. We asked the class to help and they suggested numerous titles: How Long It Takes to Get Straw, Time for Building a Nest, All About the Female Bluebird, How Long the Female was Away From the Nest, The Time Period Between Coming and Going, Female Bluebird Comes and Goes, and Project Bluebird Watch. The girls appreciated the assistance and the episode underscored the importance of bringing problems to the attention of the class. Another problem occurred when Deidre and Nikki tried to figure out which times went under which categories. As Nikki explained, "At first we were just going to do thirty seconds, one minute, two minutes, and more than two minutes. We thought we had it all done. Then we came to one minute and twenty seconds . . . and Danielle said, 'You're going to have to round it off.' When Phyllis asked them to explain how they rounded, Deidre told about the strategy she had learned in previous years, "Well, last year we learned that if it was in the middle, like fifty or more, then it would be for the two minutes. But if it was forty-nine or less, it would be for one minute." We discussed with them that rounding is indeed based on the "middle," and then calculated the middle for one minute to be thirty seconds rather than fifty seconds. The lesson helped them see that rounding is dependent upon the context in which it is found.

Further Hypothesizing Sets New Directions

As the activity of the bluebirds continued, the children wanted to keep track of other pieces of data. They wondered what the female was actually doing inside the box, so they began to track the amount of time she spent in the box. Others were intrigued with how long the female stayed on the wire, the roof of the school, or some other location before she went into the box. Another piece of data that we had never considered was suggested by Rhiannon when we shared a video of the bluebirds as this nest-building activity was going on. Since everyone could not be at the window at once watching the bluebirds, David sat with several students as they recorded what they saw and he videotaped some of the activity. (If David had not been there, Phyllis would have tried to enlist the help of some parents.) We often shared parts of the video with the children so that everyone could look closely and interpret what was happening.

INVESTIGATING A HYPOTHESIS   Rhiannon noticed that on one occasion the female returned with a large load of pine straw after she had been gone for a long time. Rhiannon hypothesized that the longer the female was away the bigger the load of pine straw she would bring back. It was certainly an interesting relationship to pursue and so we began to track the size of the load. We realized that the use of technology—the video camera—allowed the children the opportunity to look more closely at this bluebird behavior and generate new relationships to pursue. The children estimated the size to be small, medium, big, huge, and a few in-between sizes, such as small/medium and medium/big. Several children graphed the data in different ways and offered some interesting interpretations about what was happening.

Rhiannon used a line graph to show the sequence of the loads as they progressed in a given day (Figure 4-4). The format of her graph was similar to that of the Cornell graphs that we had shared with the class. She used dots to designate specific points in time and a line to emphasize the differences between those points. She placed times along the horizontal axis so she could compare the time away from the box with the size of the load. She cleverly drew some birds along the vertical axis and put different amounts of straw in their mouths to show the increasing size of the loads: small (2), medium (4), big (8) and huge (16). When we asked her why she happened to use that sequence of numbers she replied, "We've been talking about doubling numbers a lot, and so I did it that way because it sort of looks like a small, medium, big, and huge load." Shunta said, "She probably got

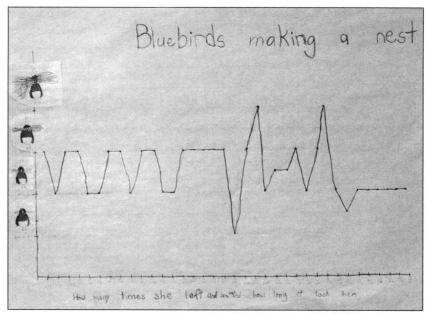

FIG 4–4   *Rhiannon's Graph of the Size of the Pine Straw Load*

the idea from the pot story," and Danielle suggested that she got the idea from Jenny's story. Both ideas were logical connections. We had read *Two of Everything* (Hong, 1993) to the class earlier in the year and the children had calculated that geometric sequence (1, 2, 4, 8, 16, 32 . . .) and also created metaphors to describe it, such as an avalanche or a tidal wave. We suspected that this pool of images was a helpful reminder for Rhiannon as she entered this new situation and sought to represent this difference in quantity in an appropriate way. After hearing this story read aloud Jenny created a story about some books that began to double and soon the owners had a whole library of books! We thought that perhaps Rhiannon might have been thinking about the base two blocks that we were using in class to keep track of the number of days we had been in school. All of these contexts were a part of Rhiannon's experience; her connection underscored for us the importance of having children create multiple stories and images for mathematical ideas.

Author's Circles for Scientific Data   When Rhiannon came to writing about her graph she had a difficult time. She didn't know how to start and what to say. Phyllis gathered several students together in an Author's Circle to discuss the matter. She invited Deidre and Danielle because they had made some of the first graphs. She asked Chris because the commentary he had written about his own graph was rather brief and Phyllis felt that he could benefit from such a conversation. Deidre read the writing she had done on her own graph and suggested that

Rhiannon begin by writing about what she did first, and then talk about what she noticed later on. It was a strategy that had helped Deidre in the writing of her own graph. Chris added, "I know some things that you can do," and described some patterns that he noticed. Since Rhiannon had shared her graph with the class recently, Deidre suggested that she "talk just like you did the other day." Rhiannon then mentioned that her theory about a relationship between the size of the load and the time away from the box did not hold true. Danielle tried to help Rhiannon further by describing that the shape of the data looked like a plateau; her comment caused Rhiannon to describe other parts of her data as valleys, plains, and mountains. When Rhiannon wrote her commentary about her graph, she clearly incorporated many of the suggestions of her classmates (Figure 4-5):

> Our class is seeing a female bluebird making a nest. Here are some things I noticed about the size of the load. I noticed that it is like a roller coaster. It starts steady and then it gets rapid. It also looks like the four physical features. Mountains, valleys, plains and plateau. I also noticed a pattern. She keeps switching from big to medium. After every huge load she brought a medium. With the plains one has 5 big in a row and the other has 6 medium in a row.

This interchange with Rhiannon showed us the importance of providing Author's Circles for students who have composed mathematical and scientific texts as well as personal narratives. We were also intrigued by her use of metaphors to describe her data because we realized that *plateau* and *peaks* (related to her metaphor of mountain) in the data were terms that statisticians actually use. At home we brainstormed other words that mathematicians use that are metaphorical in nature, such as *bell curve, square numbers, square root, sine wave, pie graph*, and *ray*. It was Rhiannon's description that caused *us* to become more intrigued with the vocabulary of science and mathematics. We learned later that the term *cell* had clear metaphorical roots. Robert Hooke was one of the first scientists to use a microscope in the seventeenth century. He studied objects under power and created careful drawings and written descriptions. He described cork, when magnified, as being full of holes that looked like little boxes. The image of boxes caused him to think of the small rooms in the monasteries of the time. Because the rooms in the monasteries were called "cells," Hooke named the little boxes in cork "cells." Later the term Hooke coined became the name for living cells, and science has used the analogy to this day (Smallwood & Alexander, 1981).

GRAPHS GENERATE THEORIES   Like Rhiannon, Jenny chose to represent the data about the size of the load but she displayed it in a different way (Figure 4-6). She counted the number of each size load for one day and then displayed those findings on a bar graph (she realized too late that the bar for the medium load was not going to fit on her paper and so she made it as big as she could and then

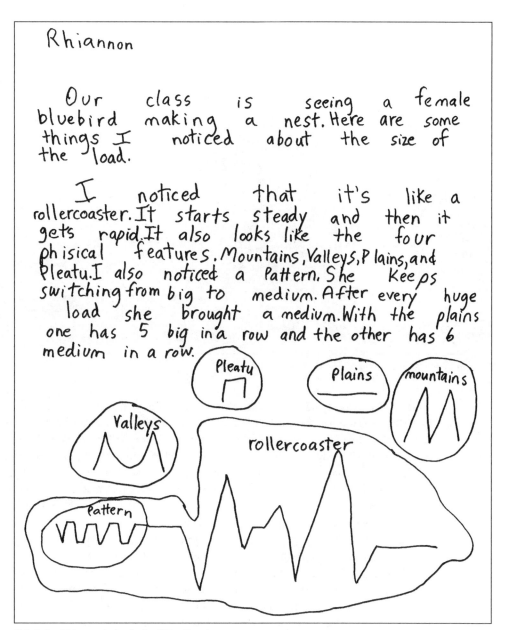

Rhiannon

Our class is seeing a female bluebird making a nest. Here are some things I noticed about the size of the load.

I noticed that it's like a rollercoaster. It starts steady and then it gets rapid. It also looks like the four phisical features. Mountains, Valleys, Plains, and Pleatu. I also noticed a Pattern. She keeps switching from big to medium. After every huge load she brought a medium. With the plains one has 5 big in a row and the other has 6 medium in a row.

Pleatu

Plains

mountains

Valleys

rollercoaster

Pattern

FIG 4–5 *Rhiannon's Analysis of Her Graph*

labeled the total for each column at the bottom of the paper so readers would not be misled). She saw that the medium load was the most frequent and offered her theory for why this was so: "My theory about the loads is that small is too little and wastes her energy going back and forth on her trips, and big is too heavy and

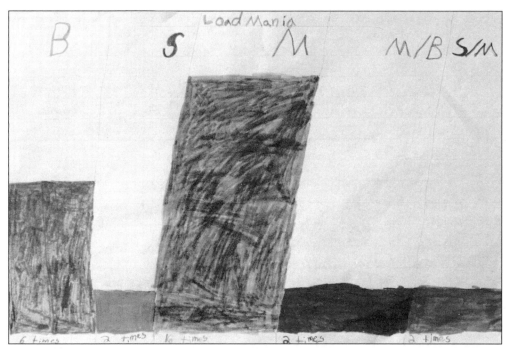

FIG 4–6 *Jenny's Graph of the Size of the Pine Straw Load*

wastes her energy flying back and forth because of the weight. So I think medium is perfect because it's not too heavy and it's not too small." After Jenny shared her theory with the class Chris replied, "I have two things to say. Even though it's a bar graph you don't really have to round off very much. You don't have to round off at all! What would happen if you put the 'big' and the 'small' and the 'small/medium' and the 'medium/big' [together], you still wouldn't get as much as the 'medium.' " Chris was referring to the rounding that Deidre and Nikki did on their bar graph about the frequency of the female's trips and realized that not all such graphs necessitate rounding. Both these graphs helped him broaden his understanding of what bar graphs can do. When Chris finished sharing the numerical relationship that he saw, Jenny confirmed it in her own words by saying, "Yeah, so what you're saying is, even if you added up all of these, except for the medium, you would still never get medium." Paraphrasing what Chris had said helped Jenny understand this new relationship in her own way. Danielle continued the discussion by asking, "Is this graph from today?" Jenny said her graph reflected the results from the day before; Danielle then predicted what Jenny might find if she went back and looked at the data from other days: "I was going to say, if you could go back and compare this one [Jenny's current graph] to the one on Monday and the one on Tuesday, those loads had to be small because she kept going back and forth all the time." Since Danielle herself had tracked the amount of time the bluebird had been away from the box, she carried this perspective of time with her as she interpreted the results of Jenny's graph. We found that by offering choices to learners about the relationships they wished to represent, we enabled learners to develop a unique perspective about the data that enriched the class's understanding. Danielle's prediction about other days of the week supported Jenny to offer a hypothesis of her own, "Maybe this might have been the first nest that she's building. Maybe she was trying out a small load for a day or so." Jenny's hypothesis then led the class into a discussion about learned and instinctive behavior in birds. Thus, Jenny's graph and the generative discussion that followed helped the class not only look more closely at the bluebirds but also pose some more global wonders about the nature of instinct in animals.

TRACKING DIFFERENT VARIABLES   Billy was another person who wanted to graph some of this data about the nest building of the bluebirds. However, he was most interested in the time that the female spent inside the box and showed those times in chronological order on his graph (Figure 4-7). As Billy, Chris, and David looked at his graph together, they first started to compare the shape of the data to other objects, such as icicles (if it is turned upside down), stalactites, flames, and a Menorah "with a big candle in the middle." David was particularly interested in the symmetry of a Menorah and commented that Billy's graph was somewhat symmetrical. Chris argued that the graph was not quite symmetrical. This brief

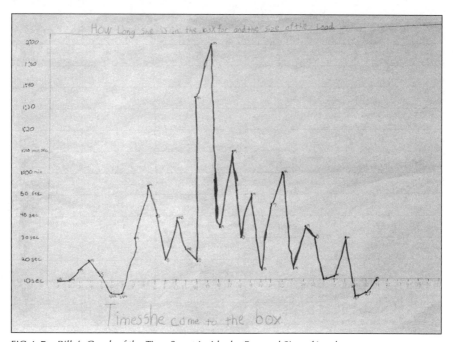

FIG 4–7   *Billy's Graph of the Time Spent Inside the Box and Size of Load*

conversation about the Menorah seemed to focus attention on the center of the graph, as the group tried to explain those times in the middle when the female was in the box for the longest times. Chris and Billy proposed a theory that when the female came back with a large load she probably spent a long time in the box. It is likely that they built this theory from the relationship that Rhiannon suggested earlier concerning the size of the load and the time *away* from the box. David recommended that Billy add the size of the load to his graph and see if his theory still seemed plausible. Later on, when Billy returned with this additional information, he shared findings that contradicted his theory, "She was in the box for two minutes but she had a medium-sized load, but the time before she had a big load and she was only in the box for 19 seconds, so maybe . . ." This new layer of information seemed anomalous to Billy, and he had to revise his thinking to form another theory that took into account this new relationship in the data. He theorized that the female alternated turns of throwing the straw in and patting it down; when she finally reached the longer time periods she then spent a substantial time in the box "patting it down and making it all nice." He drew a diagram to illustrate this theory:

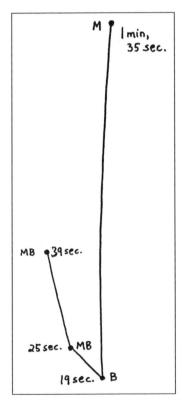

FIG 4–8 *Billy's Diagram of His Nesting Theory*

When he wrote about this theory later he explained his thinking in this way:

> She had a medium/big load and she was in there for thirty-nine seconds. Then a medium/big load but she was in the box for twenty-five seconds. Then she had a big load and was in there for nineteen seconds. Then she had a medium load but she was in there for 1:35. I think she was patting it all down. Then she had a medium load and she was in there for 2:00. I think she was in there for so long because she might be fixing it all up so she can put more in. I noticed that at the beginning there were lots of bigs and not many mediums. Then at the end there were a lot of mediums and not bigs. I think she was getting tired. Near the end I think she threw it in, then pat it down, throw it in, pat it down, throw it in, pat it down. Then she would pat it all down.

Billy recounted the anomalous data that he encountered and then suggested a theory that took into account this new information.

These three graphs by Rhiannon, Jenny, and Billy were a powerful demonstration for the class that a given set of data could be displayed in various ways. Rhiannon chose to show the sequence of the loads, Jenny displayed the frequency of the loads, and Billy showed the time in the box. Each graph enabled the children to make new insights about bird behavior by generating theories to explain each set of data. We also noticed that this interest in collecting data arose because the children were in awe at how fast the female kept returning with a mouthful of straw. It was this fascination with the natural world that always seemed to provide the initial and sustaining force for the investigations which the children pursued. In this way we did not force mathematics into this study of birds in some artificial manner, but allowed it to emerge quite naturally because the children looked closely, had questions, and wanted to know more.

The Spiral of Observation, Wondering, and Hypothesizing Continues

The female bluebird spent about eight days building the nest. We weren't sure when all the eggs were laid exactly, but we did observe both the male and female bringing food about three weeks later. The nestlings then fledged about two weeks after their hatching. However, it was the children's fascination with the feeding of the babies that prompted us to collect even more data. The children could often see what the adults were bringing for food, but when they used a pair of our binoculars, they could recognize the type of food even more clearly. This interest led the class to keep track of who was bringing the food, the kind of food, the time they were bringing the food, and where in the yard they were landing before they brought the food into the box. We and the children accumulated this data for about four days and then made copies of it so the children could look at it more closely. Next we conducted a whole class Author's Circle to brainstorm what kind of information might be interesting to compare. We felt that the earlier graphs provided some important demonstrations for the rest of the class about the many possibilities for displaying data. As the children examined this current data, which focused mainly on the feeding behavior of the adults, they suggested some interesting relationships. Amanda said that the class could examine what kind of food the adults brought. David responded, "Yes. Or you could look at what kind of food did the male mostly bring. Or the female. Or did they bring different kinds of food at different times of day? These are a whole series of questions that we could look into that relate to food." We found that an important role of the teacher is to extend initial suggestions as well as narrow the focus of more general ideas. It is this same kind of spirit that pervades a good Writer's Workshop and we were employing it to explore the possibilities in a mathematical realm as well.

FINDING WAYS TO GRAPH AN INTEREST   We asked the children to graph any relationship that they found interesting. We encouraged them to display the data in whatever way made the most sense to them. They were also expected to write an analysis of the graph that focused on what they had learned about the bluebirds. The children chose a variety of topics: times that the bluebirds brought the food, the kind of food that each adult brought, the sequence of the adults as they brought the food, a comparison of the workload of the male and female, the amount of time that each adult was gone looking for food, where the adults landed before entering the box, the amount of time each adult spent perched on the wire before entering the box, the gliding pattern of the bluebirds as they flew to the box, and several graphs on the fecal sac—a saclike membrane that the nestlings discharge that contains the feces of the young birds. There was a graph on the amount of times each adult removed this sac from the nest, a time-series graph on the relative size of the sac, and a graph on the amount of time between the removal of each sac.

One of the demonstrations that these graphs provided was the multiple ways that a given set of data could be displayed. For instance, the feeding behavior of the adult bluebirds was one such example. Brent decided to compare not only the number of times that each adult fed the babies but also how those times compared across different time periods. He used morning, afternoon, and night as his three time periods (Figure 4-9). He was able to use data from the evening time period because we adults had done some observing at night so the class could learn more about this whole process. On this particular day he noticed that "The female does most of the work. In the morning the female does almost all the work. The male does six (feedings) in the morning and afternoon but at night he does five (feedings)." The children wondered why the female was so active in the morning while during the rest of the day both adults did about the same amount of work. Some suggested that she became tired as the day progressed. Brent explained, "I thought the female had more energy in the morning. She went to the box 34 times in the whole day, so she'd be pretty tired by the end of the day." Shannon had another

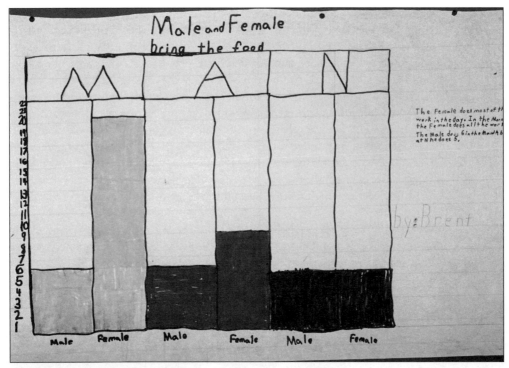

Male and Female
bring the food

M A N

22 21 20 19 18 17 16 15 14 13 12 11 10 9 8 7 6 5 4 3 2 1

Male   Female   Male   Female   Male   Female

The Female does most of the work in the day. In the Morn the Female does all the work. The Male does 6 in the Mon and 6 at N he does 5.

by Brent

FIG 4–9   *Brent's Graph of the Feeding Behavior of the Male and Female*

theory based on the graph that she completed on a different aspect of the data. She looked at where the adults perched before they entered the box with food; she found that the female usually landed on the wire but the male perched in various locations, such as the roof or the meal tray. Her theory was that the male flew to different locations so he could guard the general area from predators. Brent's graph seemed to lead the class to this same conclusion. Perhaps the male spent less time feeding the young and more time guarding the territory from predators.

David suggested that another way to display some of the information was on a piece of adding tape. Several children used that idea to record their data and made some additional insights about feeding. Tony found that on another day the female was much less active feeding the young in the afternoon and concluded that the female needed to conserve her energy so she could do a better job of keeping the babies warm at night: "My theory is it gets colder at night and she keeps the babies warm."

DECIDING WHAT TO GRAPH   Chris focused on the popularity of the meal-worms that we put out on a tray every day, a rich source of protein for the adults to feed their young: "I noticed three times the bluebirds ate a bunch of meal-worms. I also noticed in the middle of the mealworms they brought back insects or worms. I think they didn't continuously get mealworms because we ran out." Chris wished we had kept track of when we put the mealworms out, and how many, because he wanted to know how quickly they ate the mealworms and at what times. We were learning that another legitimate problem of scientists is to de-cide which information to track and which to let go (a problem of teacher-re-searchers as well). The data that scientists collect and display may look clean, pol-ished, and complete, but the reality is that much of the most interesting data was never collected at all. We felt that these lessons were valuable ones for the children to experience as scientists in their own right. They were realizing that all data is in-complete, and that sometimes the best questions are the ones they never asked.

DIFFERENT PERSPECTIVES ON SIMILAR DATA   Jenny also used a piece of adding tape to display some of the data (Figure 4–10). As she began to record her data she found she had to revise her thinking as more data was revealed, "The first day it looks like there's more females than males, and I thought that maybe the male was just being lazy but then when I saw the second day I thought that maybe one day

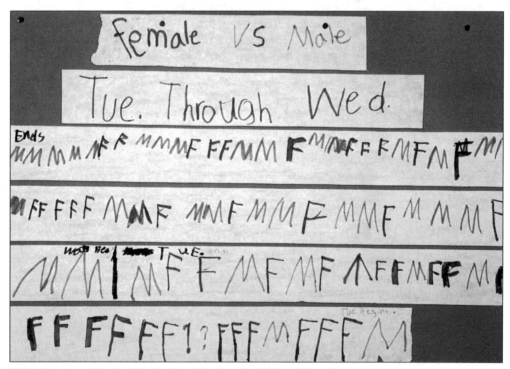

FIG 4–10   *Jenny's Graph of the Feeding Behavior of the Male and Female*

the female does it, and the next day the male does it." When Phyllis asked her what she was now wondering about Jenny replied, "I was wondering why the female did so much on Tuesday. And I have a theory about why the male didn't do so much on Tuesday. He maybe was guarding the nest more of the time than getting food." Of course, her theory paralleled the theories that Shannon and Brent had formulated as they analyzed their own data. The children were seeing that similar theories can be corroborated by considering the different perspectives that various people take on a given phenomenon.

Rhiannon displayed the feeding habits of the bluebirds as well but she focused on the kind of food that each adult brought (Figure 4-11). When she wrote her analysis she admitted that some of the results surprised her: "The bluebirds brought more mealworms and I thought they would bring more worms. The female brought fifty-five [mealworms] and the male brought seventy-seven. They're both double-digit numbers. I thought the female would bring more [overall] but the male brought more. The female brought 121 and the male brought 188. I think the female was watching the kids most of the time so the male brought more food to the kids." Her data gave the class a broader look at what was happening because she did not focus on just a few days; her data again confirmed the

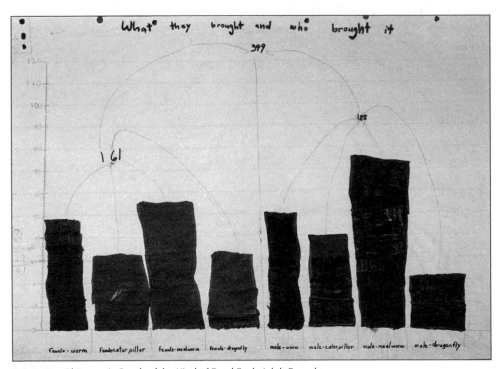

FIG 4–11   *Rhiannon's Graph of the Kind of Food Each Adult Brought*

popularity of the mealworms and showed the dragonfly as the only piece of food that the female brought more of than the male.

These graphs about the feeding behavior of bluebirds revealed some interesting insights that the class could not see in the daily charts that they had been keeping. Each visual display highlighted unique relationships for further analysis. A good example of this power of graphic design occurred in London in 1854 (Tufte, 1983). There was an outbreak of cholera in central London that eventually claimed the lives of more than 500 people. Dr. John Snow decided to plot the locations of deaths on a map so he could see the data in another way (Figure 4-12).

He used dots to mark the deaths and crosses to designate the area's eleven water pumps. As he examined the map he noticed that cholera occurred almost entirely among those who lived near (and drank from) the water pump on Broad Street (marked by an *x* to the right of the *d* in *Broad Street*). He ordered the handle

FIG 4-12 *Street Map of London to Show Outbreak of Cholera (public domain)*

removed from the contaminated pump and thereby halted the neighborhood epidemic. Thus, our children were learning, just like Dr. Snow, that the visual display of data yields fresh opportunities for examination and analysis.

These graphs also raised questions and theories about the roles of male and female birds. In order to interpret what they saw the children often compared birds to humans: They both communicate with each other, look for a house together (at least the bluebirds did), and raise a family. However, when the children made predictions about male/female roles based on stereotypic notions from human contexts, we questioned those assumptions. For instance, when Danielle predicted the female would probably feed the nestlings and take primary responsibilty for removing the fecal sac because that is what she saw happening with humans, we asked the class if they agreed with those role assignments. The ensuing discussion served to make the children more aware of the liabilities in making that kind of parallel. However, we did not use the birds as a framework for discussing this issue in depth. We felt that a closer examination of human gender roles was better addressed in human contexts that we might find in literature, history, or the social structure of the school.

Revising Along the Way Sharpens the Focus

Andrew wanted to keep track of "where she is before she goes in the box." He organized four columns to show the main locations that he had observed: tree, on top of the school, straight in the box, and on top of the box. He thought that he was organized for the task that he had set for himself, but he ran into difficulties almost as soon as he started. For instance, sometimes the female would land on one of these locations and then fly off, never entering the box at all. David was sitting next to Andrew at the time and asked him if he was going to record that behavior. Andrew decided that he would and created an O to designate any time she came to a particular location and then "was scared away." Another unanticipated behavior occurred when the female flew to several locations before she entered the box. David asked Andrew if he was going to record all those stops along the way or just the last stop. He decided to use an X to designate any place she landed on. He saw later that, although his X's marked a landing place, he did not indicate in what order this hopping occurred. He decided to make a single tally mark to show a location that was used only once. Thus, Andrew cleverly created a series of symbols to represent these unexpected events.

As he continued to watch the female bring pine straw to the box, he had to make some other decisions as well. David noticed that when the female flew straight into the box, she sometimes swooped from on high and on other occasions she glided low to the ground. He asked Andrew if he wanted to include that detail on his graph but Andrew declined. Andrew also observed that the male landed on the box several times and David asked him if he wanted to track how the male came to the box. Again Andrew decided not to record that piece of data. Even though Andrew declined to pursue these suggestions, it still was important to raise them. As a scientific researcher Andrew was having to decide what details to include and what to leave out. By at least entertaining these possibilities he was made more aware of the options he had as a researcher. Being cognizant of this range of opportunities is an important perspective for inquirers to have: "We heighten our awareness of what is actual by considering what is possible. We are conscious of what we do to the extent that we are conscious also of what we do *not* do . . . of what we might have done" (Donaldson, 1978, p. 97).

Being aware of what to let go and what to hold on to was a tension that many of the children had to contend with. When Tony asked Andrew, "When she got scared did she drop the pine straw and leave?" Andrew replied, "She mostly held on to it." However, Andrew did not keep track of this piece of data as well. Here again Andrew was made aware of another relationship that he could have pursued. One of the benefits of collecting data is realizing all the data that was never collected. There were other instances as well. As we looked at the video of the bluebirds again toward the end of the year Scott realized that he wanted data on a behavior that we had never tracked: The amount of time that the female poked her head out of the box before leaving and whether or not there were any predators in the area at the time. During the last few days of school William was gathering data about another behavior that he found interesting: Do the same species return to the yard at the same time each day? Both he and Scott were posing questions that were clearly built on the previous questions that the class had investigated. Yet their questions still required that they go back to the window and make further observations about phenomena that we had neglected to track. They were learning that sometimes scientists do not realize, until much later, what is truly significant. However, by reflecting upon these missed opportunities the children were forging new possibilities for future investigations. In addition, they were coming to see that science is not the clean, rational, predictable endeavor that science textbooks would make it out to be. Rather, it is an enterprise that is messy, tentative, and anomalous.

The Problem of Forest Fragmentation

The second example of this shifting nature of an inquiry investigation was the class' exploration of an environmental problem known as forest fragmentation. Phyllis had become intrigued by this problem after reading a brief article about it in some material that the Cornell Laboratory had sent the class. The article explained that certain species of birds have difficulty breeding in "forest patches." Cutting roads through forests fragments them, even though little actual acreage is lost. Phyllis wanted to know more about this problem, so when Mr. Steve Dennis, President of the local Audubon Society, came to visit our classroom she asked him if he could give any more details about this current problem.

Models as Tools for Investigating

When she asked Mr. Dennis about the issue, he hesitated. "It's a difficult concept," he admitted. "I don't know how I could show it so the class would understand." He paused a minute thinking, then reached for a stack of field guides. He spread the books on the floor so that they touched. This representation, he explained, stood for a large, unbroken forest. Next he pushed the books apart. He told us that cowbirds, which lay eggs in tanagers' nests, put the host broods in danger. Cowbirds only live in forest edges. When people cut forests into smaller pieces, they provide more places for cowbirds to threaten tanagers' chances for survival. The children followed his explanation because of his clear use of the model. Phyllis was impressed both with the nature of the ecological problem as well as with Mr. Dennis's ability to make a complex concept clear through the use of a model.

When we went home that evening we discussed this problem of forest fragmentation together. We wondered if we could develop Mr. Dennis's model further in order to investigate what really happens to the perimeter and area of these forest patches when they are divided into smaller pieces. We took some graph paper, cut out a 16 x 16 cm square, and began to divide it into smaller pieces. We knew that the number of places for the cowbirds to enter this original patch of forest was going to increase, but we wondered how dramatic the change would be. We wanted to look for mathematical patterns in the results as the number of cuts to the forest continued.

We had clearly been caught up in the intrigue of this problem, both from a mathematical and an ecological perspective. We could not separate our curiosity and questioning from that of the children. We were coming to realize that the role of the teacher as an active learner in an inquiry investigation is just as important to recognize as the learning of the children themselves. We wanted the children to join us in this investigation—not because we wanted to "fit in math," but because we felt the model highlighted particular features of a problem that we and the children found interesting. Although we obviously knew in advance what the mathematical pattern was, we did not know how the children would interpret the results or how they would extend it. We could not anticipate their questions, their personal connections, and their emotional responses. We knew that our model was based on certain assumptions, such as the size of the initial forest patch, and the manner in which it was fragmented. We were anxious to see how the children might want to change some of these attributes and extend the problem in other ways. Thus, we were planning an experience for the children without predetermining what was going to happen every step of the way. This is another part of the role of the teacher: to plan learning experiences that are open to individual interpretation, extension, and revision. In this way the mathematical model can become a catalyst for opening up new questions and generating different perspectives rather than closing down the conversation and shutting off further exploration.

The next day we shared the model that we had developed with the children. We had each child cut a 16 x 16 cm "forest" and count the number of squares on the outside edges to determine the number of entry points (or what we later called "attack points") for the cowbird. The children found the total to be 64 by using various strategies: counting the squares one by one, counting one side and then adding that number four times, or multiplying the number on one side by four. We encouraged them to draw small arrows on each "point of entry" to keep an accurate count. We then asked the children to cut that square in half, creating two 8 x 16 rectangles, and predict if the cowbird would have more of fewer entry points into the forest. Chris referred to the overhead pieces that we had used to assist him in explaining his thinking: "They'll be more [entry points] because if you put the two pieces together there's not going to be any arrows there," pointing to the line of division that we had just made with our first cut, "and so there's to be 64 [entry points]. But if you put them like this," showing the two separate 8 x 16 rectangles, "that's another 32." The model helped Chris see this sudden advantage for the cowbird; since he knew the length of each side to be 16, he saw quite readily that doubling that number would give him the projected increase.

Learners are able to see these kind of relationships because they can move the pieces of a model around and note the consequences of certain movements in a rather fluid way. For other children this increase in the number of attack points was not as obvious. Andrew predicted that "There's going to be less because the bottom parts [of the two 8 x 16 rectangles] are smaller." He saw that the width of the two rectangles was shorter than the length of the original square, and therefore predicted that the number of entry points would be fewer. However, as he spent more time working with the model in class, he revised his thinking. After this brief discussion we invited the children to investigate this problem on their own and see what they noticed; we felt that this exploratory period would give them the opportunity to test out these predictions in their own way and come to grips with what they saw happening.

Using a Mathematical Model to Understand the Plight of Tanagers

As the children began to investigate the problem together they found the following pattern:

Size of Forest Patch	Entry Points for Cowbirds
16 x 16	64
8 x 16 (2 pieces)	96
8 x 8 (4 pieces)	128
4 x 8 (8 pieces)	192
4 x 4 (16 pieces)	256

The model helped the children better understand the plight of the tanagers. Scott wrote in his journal, "The forest gets smaller. The cowbird has an advantage to lay her eggs." Amanda wrote, "I noticed that when I had cutted them in four squares you would have a larger amount of exits (entry points) for the cowbirds." Stephanie focused on the dwindling size of the interior as well: "I looked and counted the arrows, 32 + 32 = 64, then 64 + 64 = 128, and it's like having more and more and more birds coming, and the box (the interior space for tanagers) is getting smaller and smaller and smaller."

Cortney related the mathematical pattern to the problem of a limited food supply: "I noticed the littler the square is, the less food they get because the birds don't like to be squooshed, so they spread out (i.e., try to find another habitat). Birds have feelings too and they feel uncomfortable when other birds are too close sometimes. The bigger the box is the more food they get because they're spreaded out, and what they eat there is more, and there's space." Jonathan used metaphorical language to describe this increasing number of cowbirds: "When the forest was whole it had 64 cowbirds to attack the other birds. When we cut it in half, it's like they sent out a newspaper that said, 'We have found nests.' Then 48 more cowbirds came to attack the other birds. When you cut the forest in two halves (i.e., cut the halves into quarters), they sent out another newspaper that said the same thing. Now there is 128 cowbirds to attack the other birds. What if the cowbirds sent out another newspaper. I wonder if the other birds (tanagers) teared down their nest, what would the cowbirds do." He also concluded his journal entry with two wonders. First he wrote, "What would this number pattern look like if it kept going?", which was one of the choices that we offered the children to pursue the next day. Jonathan's other wonder, "What would the cowbirds do if the tanagers just destroyed their own nests and left the area altogether?" pertained to the more general question regarding what tanagers do when faced with this problem and what cowbirds do in response. This was a question that we continued to investigate even after this simulation experience was over. We found that some species incubate the eggs of the cowbird, others take the egg out of their nest, or build a second nest, and some abandon their nest altogether.

Other children wrote additional observations and wonders. Rett described the decreasing area for tanagers, "I notice that when the forest gets fragmented the cowbirds get more places to attack and the tanagers get squished. One of my wonders are do the cowbirds like to put the eggs in other different species of tanagers, as well as other birds." Rett's query again highlighted the children's interest in knowing more about the behavior of cowbirds as well as the behavior of other kinds of tanagers. Rett spent long hours outside of class reading about bird behavior, memorizing various species, and observing bird activity in his backyard. Thus, his personal interest in learning about different species of birds led him to raise a more specific question for the group to consider. We had lumped all the tanagers together (scarlet, summer, and western) but Rett was questioning one of the assumptions of our model, namely that it would apply to all species of tanagers, and he was urging our class to examine these finer distinctions. Here again it was a child that caused us to look more deeply at a scientific problem. We were learning that perhaps one of the liabilities of a model is its potential to simplify problems that exist in the real world. Rett was calling us to return to the real world of specific species and relate that knowledge to our model.

In reflecting on Rett's insight, we were reminded that meteorologists share a similar struggle when constructing models to predict the paths of hurricanes. Meteorologists constructed six to eight models of hurricane Erin (*The State*, 1995) based on different sets of variables, and then had to decide which model best represented the complexity of the storm. It was difficult to predict which model was most accurate due to the many variables that they had to consider, such as the movement of low pressure systems and the location of the center of the storm. Models inevitably simplify and distort a hurricane, and meteorologists must decide which one best simulates what is occurring. Like Rett, meteorologists know that no model accurately reflects the complexity of the conditions of the natural world.

Weeks later Rett's speculation was confirmed when we received additional information from Cornell. The Lab's latest findings suggested that summer and western tanagers may not be as sensitive to forest fragmentation as the scarlet tanager (Rosenberg, Dhondt, et al., 1995). Although their "answers are still speculative," Cornell hypothesized that perhaps the summer and western tanagers may be more adapted to living in fragmented forests because "Forests in the south and west tend to be naturally fragmented or patchy, whereas forests in the Northeast historically have existed as a continuous expanse." Rett's query forced us to examine the problem of forest fragmentation more critically, and we found the problem to be far more complex than any of us had imagined. Complexity, however, is a relative issue. The new information did not seem complex to the children because it was information that addressed their current concerns.

Discussing Our Findings and Setting New Directions for Investigating

As we came together to share what we had discovered, the children described the problem in many different ways. A brief glimpse at part of the conversation helps to highlight this diversity of responses:

Brent: It's like first you have this big, humongous forest. Then people need the trees to cut down to use for paper. They come in and chop it down and then you got two smaller forests, which gives the cowbird a lot of room to come in and get the tanager. So then they need more paper, so they come back in and make a smaller forest, which gives the cowbird *a lot* of space to get at the tanager and get at its nest.

Rett: I noticed that when the forest gets smaller, the more attacks the cowbirds can have around it, and the tanagers are getting more and more squooshed, and the tanagers have no other choices to spread out, and so that's going to let the cowbirds to leave their eggs in their nests.

Jenny: You started off with sixty-four, and now you got ninety-six. And if you add two sixty-four's that would be 128, and that's the answer for the third one.

DJW: Yes, so when we reach 128 the cowbirds have twice as many places to attack.

Danielle: You know how Rett was saying that the smaller the spaces the bigger the attack places. Well, it's almost like our fractions because, like the smaller the number is, like one half, it's big, which means one half would be like a bigger space, which means more attacks. See, one half is a small number (the two in the denominator is small) but it has a bigger place to attack at. It's just like switching it around.

DJW: Yes, that's a very good comparison.

Chris: I was thinking of a "What if." What if they only cut off this much, what would happen? (He suggests an alternative way to cut the forest by just cutting off a small square from one corner of the forest.)

DJW: What do you predict you'd find if you cut it that way?

Chris: The cowbirds wouldn't have as much of a chance of getting in and attacking. What made me think of that is, I don't think if somebody comes and cuts down some of the forest, I don't think that person is going to cut down half of it.

Jenny: Since I got to 128 I tried to do sixty-four three times (earlier in the conversation she had noted that 128 was composed of two sixty-four's so she now tries adding three sixty-four's). I got 192 and I wonder if we went on, and we went on cutting, if the answer would be 192 squares. And also, I was thinking of the rain forest. If we cut down trees in the rain forest I wonder if that's why it leaves those birds in danger. And would it leave the predators more places to kill the animals?

There are several important points to make about the nature of this conversation. First, there is this varied personal response, such as Brent's connection to a paper company, Rett's concern for the tanager, Jenny's intrigue with predicting the number pattern, and so on. Second, Danielle recognized the generative nature of inquiry conversations when she noted that Rett's description caused her to make a connection to our recent study of fractions. She saw that in fragmentation, the smaller the pieces, the greater the number of attack points. Similarly, in fractions, the smaller the number in the denominator, the larger the piece (one half is larger than one eighth, even though the number two is less than the number eight in natural numbers). Third, Danielle's comparison highlights the importance of fostering metaphorical thinking. Danielle's metaphor not only enriched the group's understanding of the habitat fragmentation problem but also deepened their understanding of fractional parts. Fourth, the conversation set the stage for future directions because Chris, as well as others later in the discussion, took the stance of an inquirer by asking the crucial question, "What if?" Our mathematical model was based on certain assumptions and Chris was challenging one of those assumptions by asking what would the results be like if the forest were fragmented in another way.

As we listened to the children further and read their reflections, we found that they had posed still other "What if" possibilities:

1. What if we cut all around the edge of the forest?

2. What if we cut the forest along one edge?

3. What if we kept cutting the forest into smaller and smaller pieces?

4. What if we cut the rectangles along their lengths rather than across their widths?

5. What if we started with a bigger forest?

Jonathan and Rett exemplified this same spirit of inquiry when they asked, What if the tanagers left? and, What if we considered all the species of tanagers? Challenging the assumptions behind any mathematical/scientific model is a crucial stance that inquirers must take. The history of scientific thought is nothing but a trail of revolutionary challenges to the established assumptions of the day. As scientific thinkers in their own right, the children were realizing that no mathematical model is sacrosanct; any model must be challenged, questioned, revised, and extended. It is this playful, investigative spirit that leaves nothing alone, calls everything into question, and encourages all learners to cast a skeptical glance at the group's current understandings.

After reviewing the children's "what if" possibilities, we clustered their ideas into three categories that we listed as choices on the board. The class spent the next day investigating one of these choices, and writing and drawing their ideas in their journals. Several children varied the model to find out what would happen if they cut up the forest in another way. Chris decided to cut just a small part of one corner each time and found his results to be quite different from the original exploration. He wrote, "I noticed that there is not as much of an advantage in the attack as there is for ½, ¼, etc. The tanagers get it better if we do it this way." Chris was the one who was especially perturbed by the simplicity of the original model that we had introduced to the class and now was able to find out for himself that other ways to fragment the forest produced quite different, and for him more plausible, results.

Other children created further variations from our initial model. Jenny cut around the perimeter of the square each time; she found that the space for the tanagers did not decrease as quickly because "you weren't cutting away at the middle space right away." Deidre wrote about a different variation in her journal: "I'm going to find out what happens if you cut the 16 x 16's edge." She found that the number of entrances for the cowbirds actually decreased by two as she kept slicing an edge off the forest. She was only taking into account the larger patch of forest each time, and therefore did not consider the overall loss of habitable land for the tanagers. Nevertheless, her findings did confirm what Chris and Jenny had found: Cutting the forest in alternative ways, such as on the corner, around the perimeter, or along the edge, were less threatening to the tanagers initially, but all spelled disaster eventually. It was this playfulness with the problem variables that gave the class a renewed sensitivity to this problem of forest fragmentation. (See Appendix E for the rubric used for evaluating this project.)

Sharing Our Findings with the School Community

As a way to share their findings with the rest of the school, several students volunteered to make a display of our major results (Figure 4-13). Deidre and Shannon wrote about the mathematics of the problem:

> What we did was we had a piece of paper which was 20 x 20. Then we cut it into a 16 x 16, which was sixty-four entrances for the cowbirds to get in. Then we cut an 8 x 16 (two of them), which was ninety-six entrances for the cowbirds to get in. After that we cut it into 8 x 8 (four of them), which was 128 for the cowbirds to get in. Then we cut into 4 x 8 (eight of them), which was 192 entrances for the cowbirds to get in. After that we cut a 4 x 4 (sixteen of them), which was 256 entrances for the cowbirds to get in. What this means is that the littler you cut down the forest, the more entrances the cowbirds will have.

Their written text complements the visual display of the pieces of graph paper model and explains the meaning of these numbers for the life of the tanager. Danielle also contributed to this project by writing a description of the nature of the problem between the cowbirds and the tanagers:

> A man came from the Audubon Society and talked to us about birds. Two birds that he talked about were the cowbirds and the tanagers. He said that the cowbirds did not hatch their own eggs. What they would do is lay them in another bird's nest. One bird is the tanager. The cowbird only goes into the forest maybe a half a mile, but the tanager likes the middle or the inside of the forest, too. So if there is any tanager the cowbird will attack them by putting their eggs in a tanager's nest. Then the cowbird's egg will hatch first so it can build its strength up. When the mother brings the food to the nest, the cowbird will get the food because he bullies the tanagers around, and he's like a big hog. Now people are cutting the forest up, and so the cowbirds will have more places to attack the tanagers.

Both these texts support each other in telling the story of the plight of the tanager. Danielle's piece tells about the threat that cowbirds pose for tanagers, while Deidre and Shannon's piece describes the plight from a mathematical perspective. The mathematical concepts of perimeter and area provided a helpful lens as the class focused on this real problem in the natural world.

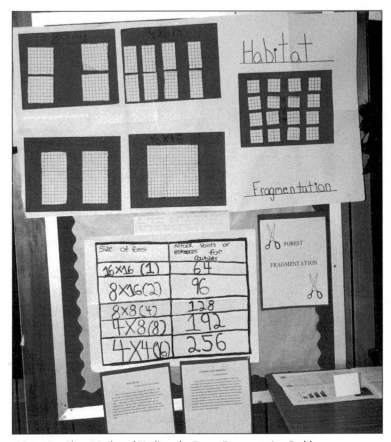

FIG 4–13   *Class Display of Findings for Forest Fragmentation Problems*

A Final Reflection

The purpose of this chapter was to describe the refocusing nature of an inquiry investigation. At times the inquiry spotlight shone on a particular problem that seemed intriguing to pursue, such as the problem of forest fragmentation. Sometimes the refocusing occurred when new observations were made, such as the nest-building activity of the bluebirds. The class explored the problem of forest fragmentation for several days (although the children revisited it from time to time during the year) and followed the story of the bluebirds for several months. The length of time is not important. What *is* important is that inquiry investigations are fed by authentic problems and compelling observations. We have found it crucial to be alert to the potential that these problems and observations hold for inviting learners down new and untrodden paths.

5 *Inquiry Builds*
Collaborative Communities

I t was February, and the class had assembled for its weekly television-style news program, "WCN: Whitin Class News." Shunta, serving as co-anchor, delivered a report that described recent bird observations. She gave a count of birds she had observed that week: "Thirty-six finches, two bluebirds, sometimes three, one tufted titmouse, two chickadees, a lot of house finches, a lot of juncos." She elaborated this list with some information about juncos that she had researched: "They (juncos) like to show their white outer tail." She also gave an editorial comment. She announced that Rett thought that a certain bird recently seen at the feeder was not a goldfinch, but a more rare, yellow-rumped warbler. However, Shunta added emphatically, "And I disagree with Rett." As she closed with, "And that's all for Bird News," Phyllis smiled to herself, reflecting on the course of events over the year that helped to create this community.

Our collective inquiry about birds had created an identity for the class and for the individuals who belonged to it. This news report and other incidents helped the adults examine the conditions that support a sense of community in the classroom and analyze the resulting benefits for learning. In turn, we looked toward the larger communities in which our class community belonged: a community of families, our neighborhoods, and the adult community of scientists. This chapter will relate the stories of those evolving communities.

Establishing and Developing Classroom Rituals

Both of us have felt that poetry is a joyful celebration of community, and we have traditionally chanted it as a classroom ritual. On the first day of school of this year, Phyllis recited the poem, "Leavetaking," by Eve Merriam, which was displayed on a large poster on the wall. She invited the children to say it chorally, and over the next few days, children took solo lines. Before long the entire class had the poem in their hearts. Phyllis added other poems to the collection on the bulletin boards regularly. The children began to suggest poems to display and read aloud. Rett found one of the first to share with the class, "The Hummingbird," (Flanders, 1983). His choice was not surprising; the hummingbirds had fascinated all of us. Most of the children's early bird observations described the movement of hummingbirds. Over the course of the year we celebrated numerous poems that reflected this interest of the class. The children checked out poetry books from the library, such as *Bird Watch* (Yolen, 1990). We read the poems aloud, and several children spent hours tracing or copying the beautiful illustrations. Inspired by these published authors, children chose to write poetry during writing time (see Chapter 2). Enjoying the beauty of language and art together as a group became an important ritual of the class.

"Naming the Day" was a second ritual that Phyllis introduced on the first day of school. David and another teacher had developed this idea when they team-taught a third/fourth grade group. The idea is also found in literature, such as *I'm in Charge of Celebrations* (Baylor, 1986). Naming the Day is a way to celebrate the momentous and the mundane events that contribute to the the fabric of the group's experience. At the end of each school day students contribute ideas for a name that will help the class remember it as a special day. Often the name describes a classroom investigation. Other names reflect the weather, a schoolwide event, a student's birthday, a read-aloud book that is completed, or a classroom guest. The names that this class chose followed the same pattern, but soon names that related to birds became regular choices: Suet Day, Tanager and Cowbird Day, Stuck Starling Day, Baby Bluebird Day.

Sharing the class bird journal became a vital part of our classroom rituals as well. Within days the children were contributing knowledge and resources from home to add to our analysis of the observations at the window. Scott, for example, brought the large volume, *Birds of North America*, so that he and his classmates could learn more about the various species we were seeing. Later in the fall several children took weekend trips and brought back news of birds spotted, and the class time devoted to sharing news and artifacts from home became dominated with bird-related events. In the spring our postvacation class meeting lasted over an hour; it focused on reports of birds and nesting behavior. If someone had new information, an intriguing observation, or a problem about birds to be brought to the class, that person was guaranteed the attention and commitment of the group.

Bird News

Perhaps it was this ongoing devotion of class time to a forum of bird-related discussions that led to Shunta's institutionalization of Bird News as a classroom ritual. Shunta had shown a keen interest in writing from the beginning of the year. She developed the first personal bird journal of the class, and she followed these observations by using writing time to research hummingbirds in reference books from the classroom library. It was Shunta's frustration with not being able to write down everything that she saw at the window that led the class to develop new strategies for taking field notes (Chapter 1). In October Shunta told Phyllis that she was writing a long story all about the class and its activities. Shunta saw that writing was a vehicle to record the collective memories of the group. It was not surprising, then, that Shunta and Danny, who sat in the same cluster of desks, developed the idea of a news program for the class. One day in November the two asked Phyllis if they could read aloud a report about the class and its activities that they had composed. "Yes, but let me read it first," Phyllis replied. She was surprised when she read the draft. It recounted various projects that individuals were doing and some personal recognitions for extracurricular activities, but it closed with an amazing rally for group spirit. Phyllis had told the class that she would be absent the following week to attend a conference, and Shunta and Danny had written about the challenge of adjusting to a substitute and the positive attitude of, "And we know that the class can do a good job." Chuckling to herself, Phyllis agreed to have the two children present their first news report to the class. Before she left for her trip, she wrote careful instructions to the substitute to provide ample time for these two students to write and prepare a second report to the class, and the ritual was born.

At first the news report was comprised of news, sports, and weather. Shunta and Danny conducted interviews for positions for reporters, and these students spent each week researching their topics and developing a report to be delivered Friday after lunch. The crew rearranged tables and chairs to simulate a studio, and before long they developed a logo and a theme song.

An incident in December inspired Shunta to add the segment, Bird News, to the show. One morning the children noticed that a finch seemed to be sleeping on Scott's platform feeder. Although the bird flew away for a short period of time, it was soon resting on the feeder again. This pattern continued for hours, so after school Phyllis called a local wildlife rescue agency. They recommended capturing the bird and bringing it to a certain veterinary clinic, which she did. The next day was Friday, so instead of telling the class about the bird's rescue, Phyllis slipped a note of "late-breaking news" to Shunta to include in the afternoon's program. The element of surprise heightened the atmosphere of a live news show. Soon Bird News was a weekly event. Shunta experimented with various forms of presentation as well. When Rett insisted that one of the new birds in the yard was a warbler, Shunta used the editorial news format quoted in the chapter opening, ". . . and I disagree with Rett." The following week Mr. Kelly visited the class as a guest speaker. Glancing out the window during our conversation, he remarked, "There's a goldfinch . . . no, I think it's a pine warbler." Rett jumped for joy, and Shunta bent over her notes, writing. On Friday's Bird News she gave a news update: "Mr. Kelly settled our argument. It *is* a warbler and not a goldfinch." A few weeks later Shunta began to incorporate graphs in her reports to show the variety of species seen during the week and the numbers of each. By that time the class had studied graphs from Cornell Laboratory of Ornithology.

A Sense of Purpose and Identity

It is interesting to note that the news program, poetry, and sharing time were not initially related to birds. However, as birds became more and more important to the children, the rituals incorporated this interest quite naturally. These rituals helped to bind the children together as a scientific community and stamp them with a unique identity. However, even though the theme of birds permeated the day-to-day life of the classroom, no one was forced to join the investigation or to commit to a required level of participation. In retrospect, we were glad that we had placed bird observation and research as an invitation during the regular writing time. We realized later that the element of choice heightened the children's sense of ownership in their learning. An experience with Nikki highlighted this idea for us. When it was Nikki's first turn to watch at the window during our regular morning observation, she admitted that she didn't really want to watch. We said, "Fine," and skipped over her name. The daily observations, sharing, and conversations continued; Nikki listened. When we reached the end of the class list, we offered Nikki a second opportunity to take a turn before we began a new round of observations. This time she agreed, commenting, "At first I didn't think birds were that interesting, but now I do." Over the course of the year Nikki showed an increasing interest in birds, choosing to focus her social studies project on the stories behind various state birds, creating one of the first bluebird graphs, and convincing her mother to buy a feeder to put outside the window of their home. When we reflected on Nikki's change in attitude, we were reminded of Frank Smith's notion of a "literacy club" (1988). Nikki did not need adults to convince her to join the class's investigation; the community served as a compelling invitation, and Nikki chose to accept.

A Sense of Community

The club feeling that developed in the class gave it a sense of purpose and identity over time (Murphy, 1995). One subtle change over the months was a growing respect for the birds. In the beginning of the year if someone saw something interesting out the window, a word of exclamation would bring a mad rush of thundering feet and sudden movement, and the birds would fly away. One day in the fall Shannon observed during writing time, and she noted in her journal that as the class grew noisier, the birds left. When the class discussed her observation, they realized that not only was Shannon deprived of observation time, but the class probably hurt the birds' chances to eat as well. The discussion served to heighten the children's awareness that their actions affected the welfare of the birds, and they began to realize the responsibility involved in having the feeders nearby. When the children noticed bluebirds entering the bluebird box for the first time, they realized that they would have to act as a team for everyone to have a chance to see the bluebird, and to ensure that the bird might feel safe enough to establish the area as a home. The class developed an agreement that if anyone saw a bluebird, she or he would quietly tell the class, and the adults would dismiss a group at a time to tiptoe to the window. Within a few days, everyone had seen the new visitors. Months later, the pair did nest, and the class felt committed to their safety. They watched for starlings, which they feared would attack the eggs, and they kept the mealworm tray stocked with food when the baby birds hatched. Billy sighed and said to Phyllis one day, "It's almost like they're our pets!" One day another teacher stepped outside to put a large muffin on the mealworm tray. She thought she was helping, but the children saw the male bluebird approach the tray, then beat its wings frantically to avoid alighting, and fly off. He was apparently frightened by this unusual food, and the children were outraged. "What does she think she's doing?" "Doesn't she know what bluebirds eat?" "Can I go out and move that bread?" "You'll have to tell her not to bother the bluebirds!" Developing a community that observed birds closely led to developing a community that cared for birds deeply.

Rallying behind the birds gave the class a team spirit, a sense of community, but it didn't mean that its members always got along. Community doesn't mean an absence of conflict, and this class was no exception. There were tears over hurt feelings, changed friendships, and worries from home. There were spouts of anger and instances of disrespect. There were trips to the guidance counselor and trips to the office, but through the ups and downs, we all were part of something that was bigger than all of us. Our shared wonder and commitment transcended the tough times of human relationships. It was the center that held us together.

Connecting Classroom Inquiry with Families

During the fall parent-teacher conferences, Billy's mother told Phyllis that they would be moving to Tennessee sometime during the year or at the close of school. Phyllis wondered how Billy felt about such a major change in his life. Her concerns were alleviated the next day when Billy greeted her with, "My mom said that she told you about Tennessee. Guess what their state bird is—the mockingbird!" The long-term study helped Billy to frame his new location with birds in mind. His brief research led him to see that he had a friend waiting for him in Tennessee. It was a friend that connected his present community to his future one. Billy's story was one way that we saw the study of birds affecting the family community as well.

Early in the year we realized that the activity behind the portable classroom influenced the children at home. Right after Labor Day we asked the children if anyone were noticing birds around their homes. Numerous hands shot into the air, and children contributed stories. Rhiannon had been watching her home hummingbird feeders closely; she had started a home journal. Other children described birds that they could not identify or birds that showed behaviors that we had not observed at school, such as a hummingbird that flew particularly high. Soon families were involved in other ways as well. Rhiannon's mother bought cardboard model birds to hang in the room. Scott's parents helped him make his platform feeder at the end of September, and Andrew and his grandfather constructed a bluebird box in November. When parents stopped by the classroom or talked with Phyllis on the telephone, the conversation almost always included a story about birds—birds in the yard at home, birds seen on trips, and visits to the library to check out field guides and other books. Jenny's mother, for example, related that while she was working on a crossword puzzle, Jenny leaned over her shoulder and suggested that she try the word *suet* to answer a clue. Jenny's mother was amazed; it was a new word to her, and it fit! Many of the families had been feeding and watching birds at home before this year, of course, but almost everyone reported an intensified involvement.

The degree of interest among families became even more apparent in December. Rett invited us to his birthday party, which was held at an indoor commercial playground. After chasing each other through numerous slides and tunnels, the group assembled for pizza and gifts. The children watched politely as Rett opened a set of mystery books, action figures, and sports equipment. Then he reached for his parents' gift. When he pulled a tube feeder and a bird-feeding guide from the box, his friends shouted, "Cool!" jumped up, and crowded around Rett to inspect the gifts. David and Phyllis exchanged glances with Rett's parents and laughed. Later they told us that they were so pleased that Rett now had an interest that he could get involved in deeply. His grandparents were giving him a birdbath for Christmas, and he had asked for a camera so that he could take pictures of birds.

We later learned that Rett was not the only one whose gifts reflected the class's inquiry. Tony's mother reported that he had asked for a bird feeder over a video game for a gift. Other children received bird feeders, field guides, bird figurines, and calendars. The connection with celebrations at home continued. In the spring Ashley's mother explained how they had altered their Easter traditions: "I purchased different types of feeders and seed for Easter instead of the traditional baskets so that we as a family could observe the different types of birds that come to our feeders."

At the end of the year we asked parents to share with us ways the children had involved families in the study of birds (see Appendix F). They wrote:

> Her science project was on the effect of color on [bird] food. I was so curious about the subject afterward I contacted a major birdseed maker and learned how color was introduced into the market.

We have read books, rented videos, and established our own bird sanctuary.

We feed them together. Whenever a new species shows up, he's quick to look them up in our bird book and we'll watch them for awhile.

Amanda has involved everyone in the house in watching birds.

She has shared with me her observations of the habits of the birds and taught me how to identify the male and female bluebirds.

We put out bluebird boxes which turned out to be pretty exciting. We all watched as the parents cased the houses and then decided to nest. Later we were all amazed to watch five little babies fly out. They still come to visit some.

She has made me more aware of them and their nature. She makes it a pleasure to watch them look for food and care for themselves.

She even involved her Uncle Sam in Hawaii—he sent her seeds of the flowers which attract hummingbirds.

Bird News from Relatives

This last comment reflected the impact of a project that Ashley inspired in the fall. One day in November Ashley reported that her grandmother in Ohio was sending her a collection of feathers (see Chapter 2). When Ashley's letter arrived, she shared it with the class. In the letter her grandmother had described numerous birds that she had observed over the years while living in Virginia, Connecticut, and Ohio. We saw Ashley's demonstration as an opportunity to collect information from around the country. When we talked with the class, we found that the children had relatives throughout South Carolina, in most of the southeastern states as well as in the midwestern, northwestern, and northeastern regions of the country. We asked everyone to write at least one relative to collect bird stories. We drew an outline map of the United States, labeled it, "Bird News from Relatives," and posted it in the classroom. As children received information, they attached Post-it notes to the map.

Although not everyone participated fully in the project, the class did gather some interesting information. Some relatives, such as Deidre's aunt, chose to relate stories from childhood. She wrote to Deidre, describing how comforting the sound of the whippoorwill seemed to her in the evenings in North Carolina. Shawn's grandmother sent newspaper and magazine clippings from Minnesota that featured many of the birds that we saw at our feeders, such as the titmouse and the chickadee (although the chickadees from the two regions were relatives, the black-capped chickadee and the Carolina chickadee).

Billy's uncle from Colorado helped show the class important information about geography as well as bird species. He wrote that he saw many of the species that Billy had named, such as the chickadee and the blue jay. However, he also saw the lark bunting and other species that were unfamiliar to our class. When the children looked for these new birds in field guides, they found that they were birds of western North America. It was interesting to them that Colorado had both eastern and western birds. We mentioned this information to Mr. Kelly of the bird specialty shop, and he explained that Colorado was on the borderline of the two general areas, so it was known for its overlapping species. We told the children what Mr. Kelly had said as we pointed to Colorado on the map. Ashley raised her hand in protest. How could Colorado be the dividing line? It wasn't in the middle of the country! Ashley, as well as many of her classmates, had expected the eastern birds to be found in roughly the eastern half of the country, and western birds in the western half. Ashley's reaction served as a springboard for the class to examine the reasons why Colorado rather than the Mississippi River would divide the two parts. What was special about Colorado? Through discussion the class realized that the Rocky Mountains were an important barrier for bird species. Western birds might be "stuck" on one side of the continental divide, and eastern birds might remain for the most part on the other side. For children in South Carolina, the significance of the continental divide can be quite abstract. Relating its role to the ranges of birds made this geographic feature relevant to the children. This issue arose only because Billy had made a connection with his uncle's personal story of the birds in his yard. The Relatives Project generated a new understanding of geography as well as gave students an opportunity to share with their extended family in a new way.

The study of the birds opened new doors for building relationships at home and between school and home. A Christmas card from Ashley showed us how powerful this part of community building could be:

> Dear Dr. Whitin,
> I'm so glad you got my grandparents and my parents involved with birds.
> Have a very Merry Christmas. I couldn't have a BETTER life! I MEAN IT.

Ashley and her classmates learned alongside their parents, grandparents, cousins, and siblings, wondering and watching together. Observing birds and sharing stories built bridges across physical distance and between generations. It was a part of community building that we had not anticipated, and we were thankful for it.

Joining Communities of Adult Scientists

Throughout the year amateur naturalists and ornithologists in our area served as resources and mentors for the class. When students talked with adults from outside the school, it became apparent that they shared a spirit of partnership in learning.

This collaborative spirit was most evident in conversations with Mr. Kelly of the bird specialty shop. Mr. Kelly's respect for the children helped them regard themselves as legitimate members of the larger scientific community.

When a few representatives first visited Mr. Kelly's store, they shared their observations about the wasted milo birdseed and asked for his advice and expertise. Over the next few months Mr. Kelly became better acquainted with some students who came to buy supplies and to chat. We adults also visited the store regularly. We related many stories about the children and their insights, and Mr. Kelly answered many questions that we asked on behalf of the class. By the time he visited the class in February, Mr. Kelly realized that the children were comfortable with complex ideas and ambiguous information. He treated them as fellow naturalists, sharing stories that demonstrated how he and other amateurs had made significant observations of birds in the state. For example, he described how a local bird-watcher had been confused by a species that looked like a Harris's sparrow, a bird whose range is defined in books as outside South Carolina. Instead of dismissing the idea by assuming that it must be another species, the bird-watcher called the Audubon Society for help. A representative confirmed the identity of the bird. The clue to the anomaly came from the habitat in which the bird was spotted—a large field that cultivated sod for transplanting to yards. The sod had provided a rich habitat for a variety of insects that supported the unusual bird's needs. "Always look for the unexpected," Mr. Kelly advised.

Mr. Kelly's remark was consistent with an important attitude of all scientists. Keeping open to other possibilities is an attitude that has given birth to many discoveries. Near the turn of the twentieth century, Henri Becquerel investigated a relationship between X rays and the luminescence of uranium salts (Best & Hein, 1976). He wrapped a photographic plate with black paper, placed a uranium salt on the package, and exposed it to sunlight. When he developed the photographic plate, he saw that the rays emitted from the salt had penetrated the paper. However, when he tried to repeat his experiment, the weather was cloudy, so he placed the prepared package in a drawer. A few days later, he unwrapped the package, and found that instead of the slight effect that he expected, there was an intense image on the plate. Like the appearance of the Harris's sparrow, this was an anomaly. Like the bird-watcher, Becquerel pursued this interesting phenomenon and discovered radioactivity. Mr. Kelly's story helped the children foster this attitude of open-mindedness that linked them to the world of scientific thinkers.

Mr. Kelly also shared stories for which he had no definite answer. He related an incident where he had seen a huge circle of buzzards surrounding two others that faced each other in the center. Mr. Kelly described his own puzzled feelings upon watching this scene. Then he added, "I want to hear what you think." The children contributed several ideas, such as a fight over a mate and a fight over leadership. He also described a time that he had seen a robin being approached by a cat. He banged on the window to try to frighten the bird away, but it didn't respond. The cat caught the bird; Mr. Kelly rescued it, and after it recovered, it was able to fly away with ease. He could not explain why the robin had not flown off initially if it were not injured. Again the children offered their ideas. Even after Mr. Kelly left, the children continued to wonder about these unusual events. Jenny and Cortney's thank-you notes reflected their continued interest:

> Cortney: Our class really enjoyed having you. I think your stories were great. Also about those birds fighting. I think it was two male birds fighting over a female bird.

> Jenny: Thank you for taking your time to come to our class. My theory about the robin was that it was probably scared of you and the cat and it didn't move.

Mr. Kelly had demonstrated to the children that adults were not storehouses of perfect knowledge. He had shown the children that he himself was not sure how to interpret certain events in the natural world. His descriptions reminded us of Rudy Mancke's remarks that science is very good at predicting and observing, but not as reliable when it comes to explaining. Again, inviting the children to join the conversation about unanswerable questions was inviting them to participate in the larger scientific community. After the class conversed with several guest speakers, we realized that one role of the teacher is to seek out local resources in order to develop this partnership. It is important for the teacher to explain to the speakers that their role is not simply to present information, but also to come to share stories, to listen, and to respond to the children's ideas.

The Cornell Laboratory of Ornithology

A second event further contributed to the children's view of themselves as legitimate scientists. We contacted Cornell Laboratory of Ornithology for information for the class, and we subscribed to their newsletter. We all learned from the materials they sent that the lab relies on amateurs around the country to gather data for them to analyze and thereby understand the changing relationships among bird species nationwide. In Project FeederWatch, for example, volunteers document the species and number of birds visiting their feeders at predetermined intervals throughout the months of November to April. Some of the results of this nationwide experiment were reported in the graphs that the children interpreted in class (see Chapter 4). In a second project, volunteers visit forests of various sizes around the country to learn more about the effect of forest change upon several species of tanagers (see Chapter 4). The children realized that it was the work of ordinary citizens that collectively supported significant understanding of ecological trends. Many of the children chose to write Cornell for more specific assistance. They felt very comfortable writing these far-away colleagues for help with their wonders. Here are a few examples:

Chris: Why does the blue jay warn other birds if it is so aggressive? How can two species of bird communicate? Isn't that like somebody from Japan talking to somebody from USA?

Lily: How do birds know what they are when they are born? Why do some birds like berries? Why do birds stay [not migrate] when it is winter and cold?

Amanda: I just wanted to ask you a few bird wonders. First I wanted to know why do some birds have red eyes. And why do woodpeckers have to go through wood to get a insect when they can go through the ground and get them? And how does a pileated woodpecker get his tongue back out to get food?

Billy: I wonder why a chickadee was peeking in the bluebird house. We do get bluebirds. I wonder why we see so many house finches.

QUESTIONS DEVELOP OVER TIME   The children's interests reflected a long history of talking, observing, reading, and speculating. Chris, for example, mentions the problem about the blue jay's reputation for aggression. The class had discussed that issue in October, and now it was January. Chris's concern with this issue helped to show us once again the benefits of a long-term study; he and his classmates could revisit ideas again and again in different contexts. It was also through a long-term study that children were able to dig deeper for more sophisticated questions over time. Chris's interest in communication reflected some recent observations with juncos, which chirp loudly whenever they fly in groups. In a similar way, Billy was concerned with the safety of the bluebirds. Amanda's wonders, on the other hand, reflect the reading that she has done alone and with the class. She had become sensitive to the fact that different species of birds show a wide variety of adaptation to their environment and for their diet. She realized that the natural world is not random; red eyes and a specialized tongue are signs of adaptation. Finally, one might dismiss Lily's thoughts about birds' knowing "what they are" as childish, but not so. If Lily had known Konrad Lorenz's study of imprinting, for example, she would have had even further evidence for raising the question. The class had learned that cowbirds lay their eggs in the nests of other species. If a cowbird hatches among sparrows, how is it to learn to separate from the host family to find its own cowbird mate? The children's questions, then, helped to show that it is the right of all scientists to raise issues that may not be answerable, or that may be answered in a new or fresh way. In fact, it is not only the right, it is the responsibility of scientists to do so.

A story from astronomy illustrates the importance of raising questions even though they may not seem to have answers. Decades ago astronomers developed the theory that stars form when strong gravitational compression creates a dense mass (Associated Press,1995). Once sufficiently dense, fusion occurs and gives the new-born star its energy. Scientists reasoned that there must be masses that did not develop sufficiently enough to become a full-fledged star, and they named these theoretical bodies "brown dwarfs." However, brown dwarfs existed only in theory until recently, when astronomers at California Insititute of Techology and Johns Hopkins University identified methane emitted by a small body nineteen light years away from Earth. Because methane is only present in cold conditions, scientists finally confirmed the "what if" posed years before. Taking risks and speculating are attitudes that all scientists share, and the children were assuming this scientific stance.

Although the children did not receive individual answers to their letters to Cornell, they were rewarded for their risks. Mrs. Margaret Barker, one of the staff members, responded by sending a packet of materials and praising the children for their inquisitiveness. Her message validated the role of the children as members of the larger community of scientists. It reads in part:

> Thank you for your thoughts, ideas, and "wonders." The staff and I will try to tackle your individual questions—although I can tell you that many of your questions are surprisingly, still unanswered. In fact, plenty of study needs to be done on birds. Scientists in many places, including the Cornell Lab of Ornithology, are trying to find answers to some of your same "wonders." Maybe someday some of you can pursue your own questions. Then, we'll all learn more about birds.

When we read the letter to the class, Brent remarked, "Gosh, it sounds like we're part of them." His comment caused us to reflect on the importance of connecting the classroom to the larger world of science. It was important to take the risk of having the children write their deepest questions and thoughts to this distant audience. The children had realized that for all scientists, inquiry is born in wonder and sustained in wonder. Secondly, amateurs can join the conversation and offer ideas, and "We'll all learn more."

CONTRIBUTIONS BY AMATEURS   As we reflected upon these relationships with more experienced scientists, we became interested in the role of amateurs in other fields of science. In the future, we will be sharing with children many stories that feature amateurs in order to demonstrate the links among communities of learners. In our reading, we have noticed that often it is someone new to a field, or an amateur, who contributes important information that leads to a change in scientific knowledge. Rudy Mancke told us an example from his own life. Growing up in Spartanburg County in South Carolina, he often caught red-bellied water snakes. However, when he looked up this reptile in a current field guide, he found that the book did not include his county in the range of this snake. Rudy collected a few species and sent the skins to the author of the book. "In the next book (edition) there was this fingerlike projection up the Broad River—and that's mine—that little fingerlike projection. Unbelievable! Here I'm a high school guy and what do I know? Why did he believe me? Because I had the specimens to prove it. There was new information."

Various experiences with communities outside the classroom built the children's confidence as theorists. The children were always eager for a challenge. At the very end of the year, Mr. Kelly extended one more invitation to the children to contribute ideas that might explain an incident that had confused and intrigued him. He had a videotape that a customer had taken about a strange event involving hummingbirds. The customer wanted Mr. Kelly to try to interpret the behavior of the hummingbirds, and Mr. Kelly in turn asked the children for their theories. The tape showed a hummingbird that was so weak it literally hung upside down on the feeder perch, breathing hard. Another hummingbird approached the first on numerous occasions, seemingly poking it with its bill until the weak bird flipped itself into an upright position and drank, only to flop back down when finished. On a few occasions, the healthy bird poked the weak one even though it was upright. Mr. Kelly was not sure what the motive for the second hummingbird's actions were. When he handed us the tape, his eyes sparkled. "I really am interested in what the children think of this," he confessed. "I'm not sure what I think myself." The tone in his voice conveyed a real respect for the children's opinions. He wasn't entertaining them or pretending to be interested in their ideas. By engaging in numerous conversations over time, both in writing and in person, he had come to regard these youngsters as competent theorists. The children studied the tape, commenting on the behaviors while they drew and took notes. They, too, were surprised and confused, but they remained undaunted by the ambiguous actions on the tape. Instead, they revised their theories as they saw new information. A sample of their comments reflects their suspended judgment:

Jenny: I think the well bird was trying to help the sick one or tell it to get something to eat. And the sick one tried to eat but couldn't go down any. I'm glad it got some food. But near the end I couldn't tell if the well bird was trying to help or not. Maybe the bird knew he was sick and let it have food but was telling it it was his territory and don't come back after.

Jonathan: I think in the beginning of the tape the hummingbird that was leaning on the feeder was very sick. My theory is the (hummingbird) is drunk to much and it got sick then when it got back up I thought it got better but it got back on the railings. My new theory is that it might of been going to sleep.

Chris: I think the male was feeding its weak mate . . . Maybe it was pecking it instead of feeding it. I think he tried to pierce his eyes. I wonder if it is raining and if it was did that have any affect on how weak he was. I don't think he's trying to feed him at all! Just attack him.

Lily: I saw a hummingbird hanging on the side of the hummingbird honey pot thing. I think he got back up but I wonder why he was hanging on the side for. Now there is another hummingbird that is trying to help the one on the side just like something like they're a family. For some reason another hummingbird keeps coming along and helping it get up but now the hummingbird was standing on it. Then another hummingbird came along and pulled it down could that be a signal. That little poor thing it looks weak and hunger like he wants some more food or that one that push him off could of been saying this is mine leave it alone its all my food.

The children drew upon numerous experiences to develop their hypotheses. The class had read that weather conditions affected the incubation and brooding durations for bluebirds, and Chris's question about the effect of weather reflected that knowledge. Similarly, Lily was well acquainted with signals as a form of communication among birds from the bluebird's wing-waving behavior. Jenny and Lily's ideas to explain the seemingly aggressive behavior may have been based on various observations. They had observed the male bluebird protect his territory during nesting, and they had watched birds of the same species (usually house finches) chase each other off the bird feeder. We had read excerpts of articles to the children about this dominant behavior at feeders. The class had seen two injured birds, one of which appeared to sleep on the feeder before we rescued it. Jonathan's change in theory may have built off those experiences.

Books about hummingbirds that we read aloud in class recounted the ferocity of this small bird; it has been known to pierce a larger opponent's eyes with its sharp beak, and Chris remembered that information. By drawing upon a wealth of information from books and direct observations, as well as the current tape, these children were developing explanations in the same way that the owner of the tape, Mr. Kelly, and professional scientists do. They also knew that it is quite acceptable to change one's thinking and to leave issues unresolved. These children and others revised their thinking in some way as they continued to observe. They realized that Mr. Kelly, like all scientists, valued a healthy conversation shared with a collegial community. Scientists thrive on debates and unresolved mysteries. Mr. Kelly had invited the children into a conversation, and they responded as legitimate members of the community of scientists, with both confidence and healthy skepticism.

The Teacher as a Community Member

During the year David and Phyllis told colleagues about this unexpected adventure with birds. The question in reply usually was, "But did you know a lot about birds before you started?" We admitted that although we had feeders and field guides at home, we had never studied birds this closely, particularly bluebirds. We had to learn along the way with the children. "Then how did you plan? How did you *teach*?" These questions implied an unspoken dichotomy: Either the teachers are teaching planned, specific content, or they're letting the kids do whatever they want. Our year-long, shared inquiry gave us the opportunity to examine the role of the teacher more closely, and we found that neither of these extremes was true. Instead we found that inquiry is not something we do *to* students, but it is fostering a way of living for all learners, including ourselves. Rudy Mancke offered his perspective on this role of the teacher.

> I do workshops for teachers and I know what they often are thinking. They're thinking, here's this guy who does this TV show and knows all this stuff. Of course he's going to think that it's wonderful to use all this in the classroom, but I don't know enough to do it. I tell them as we begin, 'If you look at the world that way you're never going to accomplish anything in your life. I would have never gotten married if I had waited until everything was just right, and I certainly would never have had children if I waited until everything was just perfect. It doesn't happen. That's just an excuse.' You start where you are now and go from there, and you make no apologies. You tell your students, 'I don't know the names of all those birds yet, but I'm going to find them out.' There's nothing wrong with that. That's wonderful.

Teachers as Learners

Part of the benefit of not knowing what to expect at the window was that we, as adults, were constantly surprised along with the children, and surprise is a close cousin of wonder. We put the feeders up initially hoping to attract a few birds close to busy school buildings. We were amazed not only that the hummingbirds visited the feeders, but also that we could see them so well. Excitement in the room was contagious, and we adults hurried to the library to learn more about these tiny creatures. We devoted time to read aloud facts that seemed unbelievable, such as a hummingbird's taking thirteen kittenlike laps for every second of sipping nectar. This was the same spirit we felt throughout the year when we learned that chickadees store sunflower seeds in the bark of a tree, a duck feather dipped in water stays dry to the touch, and that a parent bluebird removes the nestlings' waste in membrane-encased fecal sacs. Our wonder led us to write for resources, visit libraries, consult experts in the field, buy equipment, strike up conversations with strangers, and spend hours looking out our windows at home. When we stepped back and thought about our own actions, we realized that we had underestimated the significance of our excitement and insatiable appetite for learning. Unconsciously, we were mentors of inquiry, and the children learned quietly from our demonstrations.

At the same time, the children realized that if we, too, were learning at the window, they could be valuable resources for us adults as well. Because we took their ideas seriously, they believed in themselves as scientists. For this reason, it was important to share not only our discoveries, but our own questions and fascinations with the children. A good example of this co-learning relationship occurred when the children became concerned about a chickadee that entered the bluebird box during the winter. Phyllis asked Mr. Kelly if the chickadees posed a threat to the bluebirds, and he replied, "No, chickadees are rather shy." Later when she thought about his statement, she was puzzled. On many occasions chickadees had seemed quite brave. In fact, one day Rhiannon stayed after school to show her mother the feeders, and while they were outside with Phyllis, two chickadees perched in the tree nearby, chirping as if to ask for food. The next day Tony and Shunta shared the same experience: "The chickadees were talking to us!" Phyllis wrote about this anomaly in the Wonder Journal and shared it with the class. A few days later Shunta announced that she had something to share. She picked up a class field guide, turned to the page describing chickadees, and read aloud portions of the text, which described the chickadees as brave. When she finished reading, she stated confidently, "I thought this would help answer some of Dr. Whitin's wonders." Shunta helped Phyllis and the class see that chickadees might be brave toward humans but shy around most birds.

This incident showed us an important aspect of the teacher's role in the community. Shunta had been reading with others, in this case, Phyllis, in mind. Because the class shared their wonders and anomalies in a public way, they came to look out for the welfare of one another's personal interests. It didn't matter if the person in need was a teacher. We came to realize the importance of sharing the limits of our adult knowledge with the children; it is a way to join people of all ages into a larger community of learners. Shunta was not afraid to share with her teacher information to help her, and by doing so, Shunta was a legitimate scientist. Phyllis was not afraid to ask for help; it identified her as a learner in the classroom.

Teachers as Decision Makers

We adults also realized that we were immersed in a second inquiry apart from our study of the birds. During the entire experience, it was our role to study the processes of learning in this context. We needed to analyze conditions that were likely to foster healthy conversations, ongoing investigations, and new directions for exploration. Our continual analysis helped us decide when to highlight an anomaly, and when to abandon our agenda in order to listen more closely to the children.

One of the first decisions that we had to make was whether or not to have field guides in the room on the first day of school. We decided against stocking the shelves with resources. We were afraid that the children might rush to find the appropriate label for a bird, and conversations would stop. We felt that without conventional labels, children would be forced to describe what they saw, and these descriptions would encourage other children to look closely at the window for more information. We also felt that if children observed, sketched, wrote, and shared first, they would better understand the need for various resources. Richard Feynman (1988) warns:

> You can know the name of that bird in all the languages of the world, but when you're finished, you'll know absolutely nothing whatever about the bird. You'll only know about humans in different places, and what they call the bird. So let's look at the bird and see what it's *doing*—that's what counts. (I learned very early the difference between knowing the name of something and knowing something.) (p. 14)

We didn't want the children to "know the name of something," we wanted them to "know something." We began to define our role as discussion leaders, extending the children's descriptions with questions like, "What do you mean by 'peck?'" or "Who can describe the hawk's flight in another way?"

At the same time, we were aware of the value of labels. Labels are an efficient means to move the conversation forward so learners can talk about other things; we don't want to have to keep explaining ourselves or we wouldn't accomplish anything. Stephanie helped to point out this value one day in September. William had observed both house finches and cardinals while they ate. He was very interested in their eating behavior. When he read his journal entry to the class, Stephanie complimented him, "I liked that you told what kind of bird it was; we didn't have to ask." Stephanie realized that labels save time, and by naming the species, the children could devote the conversation to the current interest of the class. Thus, the decision of when to ask for description and when to sanction labels is a contextual one. We were learning that in order to encourage inquiry, teachers need to develop a sense when learners are hiding behind labels and when they are using these labels to get on to more important issues.

There were other occasions when we felt that it was extremely beneficial to use scientific language. We decided to use words such as *theory* and *hypothesize* from the very beginning because we wanted the children to see themselves as legitimate scientists. We chose to respond to the children's comments, such as, "I think birds like the rain a little because it's like a shower," with, "That's an interesting theory. Does anyone else have any evidence for Danielle's theory about birds and the rain?" Choosing *hypothesize* over *guess* and *theory* over *opinion* is a way to treat the children's ideas with respect. Another related benefit of this intentional use of words is to define us as a scientific community. We purposely used words such as *wonder, investigate, explore,* and *predict* to portray publically the active, constructivistic nature of our work as a community of scientists. We found that children would then use this language themselves to describe their thinking. Thus, teachers can play a key role in the development of a classroom's language and identity.

Encouraging Community Support

Another role of the teacher was to foster a positive tone of community support. As we described in Chapter 1, we established the ritual of sharing appreciations and questions for the daily journal recorder. In time this practice led to the students' publicly acknowledging one another for their contributions in developing theories. We realized that the children might not value the process of learning from conversations unless we encouraged them to reflect upon this process. From time to time throughout the year, we would close a conversation with the request, "Put your hand up if you thought of something during this conversation that you had not considered before we talked." When the children raised their hands, we would invite several to acknowledge a classmate as an inspiration. We commented at the end of these sessions, "That's why we share ideas in a group. We always learn something new by listening to one another's ideas. We could never have made these discoveries or observations alone." At the same time, we adults would often recognize one of the children for their inspiration to our thinking. When we acknowledged the children in this way, we moved back into the role of learning with the children.

Another part of fostering generative conversations was to invite personal connections to an event, especially when we were generating theories (Chapter 3). We found this role, too, to be a delicate balance. On some occasions, especially at the beginning of the year, some children would use the opportunity to tell tangential tales that drew more attention to the speaker than benefited the understanding of the group. One day, for example, the class was brainstorming ideas for projects. They were considering learning more about which birds preferred which seeds, how birds kept dry in the rain, and other wonders. At one point the children discussed if birds liked the breeze, and they suggested setting up fans to test this idea. Shawn protested that the birds might get hurt by the fans. One of the children, inspired by the mention of injury, recounted a tale about his brother's being bitten by a goose. He paused from time to time, and the class responded with giggles and exchanged glances. At one point David prompted, "And what were you wondering?" He answered hesitantly, and Phyllis commented that his story might address the issue of which birds were the bravest. She reminded him that we had read aloud about aggressive hummingbirds, blue jays, and mockingbirds. She concluded, "We might want to find out more about which birds are the bravest. Which ones don't get frightened away easily." In this case and others, we found that sometimes the role of the teacher in the community is to send a double message: Although it is beneficial to extend ideas by bringing individual experiences to the attention of others, it is also important to remember the group's purpose.

It was the responsibility of the adults to evaluate the potential of classroom events, and to decide when to highlight an anomaly for discussion, a strategy for research, or a tool for extended observation. Sometimes opportunities would arise naturally from the children, but sometimes we decided to bring something to the children's attention ourselves. The children naturally wondered why the outer diameter of an eagle's nest was so large, in contrast to its inner depression, and we encouraged the children to create theories about their observations. On the other hand, David noticed that the male bluebird usually faced the sun when preening, and he invited the children to wonder along with him in conversation and in writing. When Nicholas and Scott mentioned that they had learned different information from two field guides, we knew that we needed to take the opportunity to talk with the whole class about the value of using multiple resources. Without this opportunity, we probably would have distributed various field guides to the children and asked them to compare them as part of a reading minilesson. Another example arose when the bluebirds began to build their nest, and we provided a stopwatch and demonstrated ways to record nesting data. As children noticed new details, such as the size of the load, they expanded the observation chart. Once again the teachers shuttled back and forth between supporting the learning process and immersing themselves as co-learners in the investigation.

Celebrating Community

One day the district science coordinator was visiting the classroom. The children escorted her to the window, identified species at the feeder, read to her from the class journal, and explained the poster they were creating about forest fragmentation. She remarked to Phyllis before she left, "It would be wonderful if these children made a video about the birds." The idea sounded intriguing. We had used the video camera to capture some of the events in the yard, and when the bluebirds began nest building, we captured long segments on tape. What better way could we share the story of our bluebirds with a larger audience. Despite our lack of experience with video production, we talked with the children and decided to take the risk. *The Bluebird Story* became our celebration of achievement (Peterson, 1992). With the help of the director of a middle-school television studio, we selected segments of tape that depicted courtship (preening and wing-waving), nest building, feeding, and fledging. The children narrated the film using journal entries, graph commentaries, Wonder Sheets (Chapter 3), and transcripts of conversations. Many of the narrated descriptions reflected long-term interests. Amanda had been interested in feathers and their oil content since October; she described the preening process while the film showed the male bluebird preening. Jenny had created a theory to explain the female's choice of size of a load of nest material (Chapter 4), and she narrated a clip showing the female making successive trips to the box. Andrew had constructed the box with his grandfather, so he opened the film describing his contribution to the story. When the film was completed, it showed how one class had learned so much together as a community, yet within that shared knowledge, each person was celebrated for individual interests and observations. Seeing their names scrolled on the screen, the children jumped and cheered. The film served as one more way to validate the class as a community, yet still recognize them as a collection of unique, accomplished scientists.

The class invited parents, Mr. Kelly, and Andrew's grandfather to a special evening showing. Later the school broadcast the video on closed circuit television for the benefit of the school community. The media specialist made a duplicate copy for Mr. Kelly, who played the film at his store, where members of the community could enjoy it. Once again the class community spiraled out to family members and to the larger club of adults who shared their interests.

A Final Reflection

Elliot Eisner has argued that schools are "cultures of opportunity" (1992, p. 592). When we reflected upon the role of the varied communities in our inquiry investigation, his statement became even more meaningful to us. We realized that the class became a unique culture that shared a common language, common rituals and celebrations, and a common commitment. The class regularly shared entries from the Bird Journal and developed a segment about Bird News to include in the weekly "TV" report. They recited poetry about birds, shared questions about bird behavior, and constructed theories to explain their current observations. There was a commitment to ensure the welfare of the baby bluebirds, to support each other in identifying unknown species, and to read with the interests of others in mind.

We also began to rethink the definition of "opportunity" as it pertained to our classroom community. Both adults and children had the opportunity to take risks and share anomalies, such as wondering how birds know what they are when they are hatched, or explaining the unusual behavior of two hummingbirds at a feeder. Class members had the opportunity to pursue individual interests, such as Amanda's fascination with the oil content of feathers and Ashley's intrigue with comparing birds in different states by corresponding with her grandmother. There was the opportunity to invite others—such as nearby parents, an uncle in faraway Colorado, the owner of a local bird store, and the president of the community Audubon Society—to join the scientific club. These were the opportunities that lay within the culture of our classroom. As the school year ended, we all left to travel down our individual paths, but we carried with us the memories of a community and the values of a culture that we had forged together.

6

Inquiry Results in Changed Visions

I nquiry learning changes how people view the world. It certainly changed us, students and teachers alike. Rudy Mancke agrees with this changed perspective, saying, "To me, that's what education is supposed to do for you. It is supposed to give you views of the world that you somehow could not get, for whatever reason, on your own. That's what schools are supposed to do. If they do not do that, if they do not change the perspectives of students, then they are of no value." He further elaborates: "The idea of making discoveries on your own—you cannot beat that. When you work on making connections then kids all of a sudden start seeing things that they would have missed otherwise. They are better observers. When you give people an interest in something other than themselves— that, in and of itself, is wonderful. It makes their life better; it makes every person they meet for the rest of their life better because they have a broader view of the world. We need this; it's essential." If we use Rudy's criterion of a changed vision of the world as the benchmark for real learning, then what can we, as teacher-researchers, point to as evidence that this study of birds changed our vision and our students' visions? We have organized this chapter around key indicators that we feel reflect this changed perspective. Some of these changes involve the benefits of a long-term study, the nature of scientific knowledge, the role of tension in learning, and the role of models in facilitating understanding. Finally, we conclude the chapter with a discussion of a sense of wonder, which permeated this study throughout the year and caused us to reexamine its central role in inquiry learning.

Signs of Changed Visions in the Children

Throughout this book we have related ways the children's words and actions reflected change in their lives. Ashley and her grandmother grew closer as they shared information about birds (Chapter 2). Children described their views of the importance of conversation in generating theories and building group knowledge (Chapter 3). Children received bird-related gifts from family members, and Billy realized that his friend the mockingbird would greet him at his new home hundreds of miles away (Chapter 5).

Changes from the Children's Perspective

In May we asked the children to complete a reflective questionnaire (Appendix G), and their comments enabled us to see new dimensions of their changed visions. Some of their thoughts reflected an appreciation for the beauty and wonder of nature. Stephanie wrote, "I have noticed that birds are a part of life, and if they start to sing, it's the most prettiest sound ever." Jenny learned to appreciate the many different species of birds and the variety of their eggs: "Now I go on more walks through the woods to see the different birds . . . [This year] I was surprised about all the eggs because of their colors." Nikki added, "I would look at birds on my porch. I think birds are very pretty. I see a lot of starlings and mourning doves around my house." In another piece of writing, Rhiannon wrote, "I spend my time wondering about birds."

When asked if they had taught anyone about birds outside of school, children related experiences with families and neighbors. Danielle noted, "I teach my mom and dad about birds, and also we spend time together just looking at birds . . . I tell my next door neighbors about birds because they are very interested in birds, too." William told his parents about "the best places to watch birds." Shunta spent time teaching her cousins to identify birds, "and they know more now." Amanda enjoyed reading with her parents about birds. She wrote, "I taught my dad at home where birds live and what they look like by reading." We learned about Rett's effect on his neighbors another way. He commented one day at school that his neighbor's yard was ideal for establishing bird feeders. When we visited Mr. Kelly's store a few weeks later, Mr. Kelly chuckled as he told us about his new customers, Rett's neighbors. Rett was doubly glad that he had won his neighbors' loyalty to birds; he could now observe two yards with his binoculars.

Some of the children's remarks showed a view of learning that carried beyond the school day or school year. Jonathan reported that after school hours, "I studied more, like if I saw a bird that I didn't know I would do research." Rett commented, "I am really glad I learned so much about wildlife, and I found an extra hobby." William thought that the projects "helped me as a learner, so that I can identify a lot of birds later in my life." Jonathan wrote advice for next year's class: "I would tell them that you need to watch out for strange things with birds because you might discover your future career." His comment caused us to reflect on the many occasions when the class wondered and theorized about birds' behavior and special adaptations. In a collaborative community it is possible to build a collective intrigue that fuels a lifelong interest. Deidre's comment extends Jonathan's. She reminds us with quiet wisdom of the value of varied resources, such as books and colleagues, and ongoing, careful observation: "I would tell [next year's class] that you can't give up on a wonder or a question bout birds. Just look it up, or ask friends, or just look out the window."

During the course of the year it was also clear to us that the children were viewing their world with birds as a lens. Many children chose to report on state birds for the districtwide social studies fair. When a visiting artist spoke with the entire fourth grade, it was a member of our class who asked, "Can you draw birds?" On another occasion Deidre and Danielle interviewed the principal for a writing project. The next day the principal laughed as she told Phyllis, "If those girls had not told me they were from your class, I would have known. They asked me to name my favorite bird!" Even the age-old pastime of passing notes reflected the influence of our inquiry. One day Ashley shared the calendar she received for Christmas, which featured large photographs of birds. During math class Phyllis intercepted a note that Rett was passing across the desks. It read, "Ashley, Was there any other bird calendars at Books a Million? P.S. Books A Million is the biggest book store I have ever been in. From, Rett."

Changes from the Parents' Perspective

We learned more about the children's changed visions by asking parents to complete a reflective questionnaire as well. Their comments enabled us to understand other dimensions of the children's changed views of themselves and of the world. In Chapter 5 we described that parents reported how their family life had been affected by the yearlong inquiry: observing birds together, buying bird supplies for gifts, and searching for resources together. Other parent comments gave us insights about conversation, community, and a reverence for nature and its interconnectedness.

The class had spent many hours discussing observations and generating multiple wonders and theories. We adults found these conversations energizing, but it was only when we asked parents to complete a questionnaire at the end of the year that we discovered an unanticipated effect of these discussions: Children were not only talking about birds more at home, but they were also talking differently in general. Tony's mother reported, "Tony has grown with this interest in birds, not only about wildlife, but it made him express himself more openly in other subjects." Chris's mother reflected a similar theme: "Chris 'wonders' out loud much more than he used to, and this gives us more opportunity to research together. He gets excited about new discoveries." These two children had changed their views of themselves as learners. They were taking more risks by expressing their thinking and sharing their questions aloud. In this way they were able to build new relationships with their families. Parents could better appreciate their children's reasoning and could capitalize on the opportunity to learn together. Rett's mother added that this changed view of oneself as a learner was empowering: "Rett has sparked the interest of many friends and family members which has instilled in him a sense of self-confidence and happiness." Rett had found the joy of making and sharing discoveries with his class community, and carried this joy with him as he conversed with others outside of school. Rett was demonstrating what Rudy Mancke meant when he said that the act of discovery changes learners so they are able to enrich the lives of others around them.

Other parents described how much their children noticed birds around them. Billy's mother wrote, "No matter where we go, Billy is always noticing birds." Shunta's mother saw a similar effect but from the perspective of time: "I have noticed that she would stay outside for hours at a time watching birds." How we choose to use our time, and what we choose to see around us are hallmarks of our changed priorities. Several parents described the change in terms of their children's deeper respect for the natural world. Rhiannon's mother wrote, "Her awareness of birds has also caused greater caring for them." Ashley's mother responded, "Ashley is very protective of 'her little friends' whenever we go outside as a family." William's mother noted, "William is much more aware of his natural surroundings in general, and of wild birds in particular. He seems more caring and concerned about animals and birds and their plights." Her comment caused us to recall how William had been particularly concerned about the danger that starlings posed to bluebirds. When the children had sketched scenes from the entire nesting cycle, William chose to draw the conventional red circle with the diagonal slash for *no*. Under the slash he drew a starling, and he labeled the sketch, "Just Say No to Starlings." William's view of the world had made him more sensitive to ecological issues. Although we as a class did not pursue the avenues of political action, we could see its potential through these comments. Our vision of teaching changed, and we realized that in the future we would need to capitalize on these sensitive attitudes in a systematic, intentional way.

Lily's parents emphasized a slightly different angle on her appreciation for nature. They noticed that Lily began to see the interconnectedness in the natural world. They wrote: "What shocks us is she's so interested in things like the yard insects and frogs, etc., and has talked about their effect on the bird life . . . Lily not only has learned about birds, but their habitats, etc." When we talked with Lily's parents, they elaborated upon these ideas, describing how Lily poked around the yard, observing and collecting insects and frogs. She became especially interested in frogs, and brought one of her specimens to school for the class to observe and sketch. After talking with her parents, we remembered with renewed appreciation that Lily had created an experiment with the mealworms for the bluebirds at school. She and Shannon had put both dead and live worms on the mealworm tray and checked the tray periodically to see if the bluebirds showed a preference for one over the other. (The local bird store had received a shipment of dead mealworms and had donated them to us. They could not sell them but felt the worms would still be attractive to the bluebirds.) As Rudy suggested, Lily was seeing things that she "would have missed otherwise." Supported by the scientific community at school, Lily was now making discoveries on her own. All of these parents helped to show us how their children had changed through conversational habits, observational abilities, self-esteem, and reverence for the natural world.

A Changed View of Tensions

The story of change is not complete without a description of the inherent struggles and tensions that are a natural part of the teaching/learning process. As we reflected on the year's experiences, we adults developed a changed appreciation for the role of tensions in an inquiry classroom. Tensions played a role both in the study of birds and in the evolution of our curricular decisions. They helped to guarantee that the process of learning will never be stationary or predetermined, and they helped to make us more reflective teachers.

Deciding When to Intervene

As teachers we faced the tension of when to intervene in classroom events and when to step aside. We have previously discussed (Chapter 5) the importance of our not stepping in front of the childrens' struggles: We let Shawn struggle with how to draw a circle with a straight ruler and we did not provide answers when Shunta complained about the difficulty in making quick field notes. However, behind these decisions was the tension of how to use time productively in school. Time is our most valuable resource and how we decide to use it is a tension that all teachers must face. The amount of time devoted to conversations was always a tension. Did I let that conversation go too long? Was that child's personal story just a time-consuming diversion or did it serve to give us a helpful perspective on the issue? We found that at least being aware of this tension made us more reflective about the decisions we were choosing to make. Of course, it was the context of the classroom situation that really influenced our decision about when to intervene. For instance, at the start of the year we purposely intervened in the early conversations about birds. When children shared their written observations, we set the guidelines for responding by asking, "Who would like to share what they appreciated about that description? Who has a question for the author?" We also intervened to conduct minilessons, how to use line graphs to display data over time, or how to use an index when trying to locate a particular warbler. At other times we chose to step aside, allowing the children the opportunity to graph whatever set of data they found interesting, or giving them the responsibility for sifting through resources to identify a mystery nest. We found that this tension helped us be more reflective about our intentions as teachers. We intervened in early conversations because we wanted to establish a climate of trust and respect; we stepped aside when it came to finding patterns in data because we knew childrens' sense-making abilities would support them in finding appropriate solutions. It was a productive tension that helped make us better teachers.

Deciding What to Pursue

Another significant tension that teachers and children faced was between what to pursue and what to let go. Andrew, for example, struggled with this tension when he recorded where the female bluebird landed upon her arrival in the nesting area (Chapter 4). At first the recording was simple: either the bird landed on the wire, the top of the school, or some other single location. Soon, however, Andrew faced a dilemma as the bird flew from location to location before entering the nesting box, or as she landed on the wire and then departed before visiting the box. As the data became more and more complex to record, Andrew decided to abandon some of the details to make his visual more manageable. He had learned what all researchers must learn in the field: It is impossible to keep records of all parts of an event. Researchers must make choices; some roads must be left untraveled. The danger of losing something potentially fruitful is risky, but in order to proceed, one must take those risks. Another example of this tension between what to pursue and what to let go came from William. He was in the midst of graphing a portion of the bluebird data, showing the amount of time the male stayed away from the box in between his feeding trips. He noticed a pattern of longer and shorter times away from the nest and hypothesized that the shorter times might correspond to the times we placed mealworms out on the feeding platform. His hypothesis was certainly a plausible one but we realized too late that we did not keep track of when we put out mealworms or of how many we put out. Thus, Andrew had to decide in the midst of his investigation what to pursue and what to let go while William learned in hindsight about data that might have been valuable to consider. They were both facing the inherent tension of what to pay attention to in the natural world.

Facing Choices as Teachers

We adults, as all teacher-researchers, faced a parallel dilemma in our inquiry into the learning process. Like William we realized in hindsight that we too had not tracked a piece of data that would have been useful information. We did not pursue the potential of drawing for expressing understandings about birds. Even though we certainly encouraged the children to draw throughout the study, we did not keep systematic records of these drawings or invite the children to describe the process they used to create them. Although we realized more and more that drawings were a powerful avenue for conveying observations and theories, we found that we had usually confined these drawings to a private learning experience. We did not capitalize on the drawings as a vehicle for generating group knowledge.

We also lived through a tension similar to Andrew's because we had to decide which curricular invitations to pursue and which to let go. Sometimes, in retrospect, we were glad for what we had abandoned; at other times we wondered what we might have lost. At one time, for example, we entertained the idea of collecting data on the amount of seed consumed daily, or to track carefully the seed preferences of various birds. A few students were willing to follow our suggestions, but within a few weeks, it was clear that this exploration did not hold their interest. We decided not to push this idea any further. However, a few months later, when the bluebirds nested, we made a similar invitation and the children were eager to collect this kind of data, and did so with great precision (Chapter 4). In this case we *did* decide to invest a lot of time on this curricular invitation. Both experiences addressed collecting and interpreting data, but one of the experiences was obviously more rewarding than the other. We were glad that we had decided to let one go and pursue the other. Like the children we were living a life of productive tensions.

At other times we adults were quite directive in initiating an experience, and we felt satisfied in that decision. The children would not have thought of investigating the problem of forest fragmentation through a mathematical model, but by doing so we all raised interesting new questions and generated significant insights, both into the ecological problem and into the nature of the model itself. Similarly, although we were unfamiliar with video technology, we did pursue the idea of producing a documentary video by seeking out knowledgeable colleagues. In the video production, however, there were other sacrifices. We would have liked to involve the children in more of the decision making of which clips to include and exactly how to lay out the script. Although we did use the children's written journal entries and commentaries from their graphs for the script, we as adults did decide which portions would accompany which scenes. In this case our decisions were based on time and energy. We knew we were letting some valuable learning experiences go by, but, like Andrew, we needed to make the experience more manageable.

Finally, there were potential directions that we wished we could have pursued. The children were interested in birdcalls, and we purchased a set of fascinating tapes of various calls and songs. We investigated this avenue briefly, but when the bluebirds nested right outside the window, they consumed most of our time and energy, and we put aside the idea of studying the sounds of birds. Similarly, we recognized the potential of taking political action about ecological issues with the children. At the time of our study, there was a local controversy about building a bridge that might endanger wildlife in the coastal wetlands. The children had demonstrated a heightened sensitivity to the welfare of animals, and taking action might have deepened their political awareness of ecological issues. We regret that we let that opportunity slip by. Finally, we knew that capitalizing upon technological resources, such as the Internet, would have been extremely rewarding and exciting. Reflecting upon these numerous opportunities after a yearlong study helped us understand that, in the tension of deciding what to pursue and what to let go, there are not necessarily right or wrong decisions. There are an infinite number of possibilities to pursue, and many are equally fruitful. We have kept records of these unexplored opportunities, and we have merely postponed those that seemed particularly promising. These reflections have led us to appreciate a healthy and productive tension as a critical part of our growth as inquirers.

A Changed Vision of Scientific Knowledge

We also experienced a changed vision of what scientific knowledge is really like. After living through this study of the birds so intensely with the children we realized again, but in a more profound fashion, the problem with how science is traditionally taught in school. Science is usually perceived as either "inexplicable magic or a fixed body of facts known through key vocabulary" (Tchudi, 1993, p. xi). It is reduced to the study of "dry bones" (Pope, 1993, p.158), the musty artifacts of long ago, such as the laws of gravity or the parts of plants. We realized that the problem lay in viewing knowledge as content rather than an outcome of inquiry. Dewey expressed the distinction in this way: "The record of knowledge, independent of its place as an outcome of inquiry and a resource in further inquiry, is taken to be knowledge. The mind of man is taken captive by the spoils of its prior victories; the spoils, not the weapons and the acts of waging the battle against the unknown, are used to fix the meaning of knowledge, of fact, and truth" (Dewey, 1916/1966, p.187).

Science as False Starts and Fortunate Accidents

Unfortunately, textbooks present a polished, sanitized view of science that treats knowledge as content, or what Dewey calls "second-hand knowledge," and omits the process of inquiry that served to achieve those understandings. Anyone familiar with the history of scientific thought knows that it is not a clean, linear, rational pathway to understanding, but a story of struggles and tensions: "It is a labyrinth of false starts, blind alleys, hedgehopping discoveries, fortunate accidents, brilliant insights, and crumbled doctrines" (Harrington, 1994, p.14). The children lived through this kind of halting history in their own way. For instance, there was the fortunate accident when Billy's uncle sent us information about the kind of birds that he saw in Colorado. He observed similar species that we had noted in our sanctuary, such as chickadees and blue jays, but he also saw several different species, like the lark bunting. His information led us all to question why, and we began to investigate the role of the continental divide in habitat development and selection.

We also experienced false starts; after seeing the male bluebird take a limited role in building the nest, the children predicted that he would probably assume a minor role in feeding the nestlings. However, they had to change this prediction when they observed him taking a very active role in the feeding as well as the removal of the fecal sacs. Another false start occurred when the children assumed, based on their recent observations, that milo was a seed that was not appealing to any bird. However, in talking to Mr. Kelly at the bird store, they learned that some western birds actually preferred milo and they began to wonder if bags of birdseed were made for this more general consumption. We also experienced a "hedgehopping discovery" when Rhiannon saw the videotape of bluebird activity and hypothesized that the longer the female was away from the nest the bigger the load of straw she brought back. Although this relationship did not pan out as we continued our observations, it did provide the basis for a further conjecture by Jenny when she theorized that the female learned to bring a medium-sized load because large and small loads wasted too much of her energy.

Science as Problem Solving

This view of science as an outcome of inquiry helped us better appreciate the importance of not stepping in front of the real struggle that scientists face. Unfortunately, schools have a long and dismal history of trying to make learning "easy" for children by developing stories of controlled vocabulary, teaching sequential steps for mathematical problem solving, and summarizing important facts in science. Real learning does not work that way. Instead, learners need the opportunity to struggle for themselves. Shawn had to struggle with how to draw a round nest with a straight ruler; Shunta had to figure out how to capture fleeting events in a more organized way; Ashley had to justify her language of "pecking" to describe her observation of a hummingbird. These are the kinds of struggles that bestow on children the voice and authority of scientific thinkers (Gallas, 1995, p. 3).

Another strategy for not stepping in front of the struggle is to value the role of anomalies in scientific learning. One of our roles as teachers is to keep raising anomalies within our classroom community because they are what drive new thinking and generate new theories. We shared the mystery of the cattle egret and asked the children to offer explanations to answer this strange phenomenon; Chris uncovered an anomaly when he saw numerous house finches at our feeder but the range map that he was consulting showed that they only appeared on the west coast. Eric, Ashley, and Billy constructed an eagle's nest out of paper but found it disconcerting that the rim of the nest was so large that they developed theories to explain this anomalous relationship. When children are compelled to regurgitate undigested facts, they are forced to live with nonsense. However, when they are encouraged to confront anomalies, question unanticipated results, and offer possible explanations, then they are living the lives of scientists. By not stepping in front of the struggle we nourish in learners the right to expect the unexpected, a critical stance of inquirers.

Science as Storytelling

Another changed vision for us about the nature of science was a renewed appreciation for the significance of story. In this regard we have come to see story as the overarching construct for explaining the world (Burke, 1995); rather than speak about fiction and nonfiction we need to think more about story as the vehicle for interpreting the world. Scientific inquiry "begins as a story about a Possible World—a story which we invent and criticize and modify as we go along, so that it ends up being, as nearly as we can make it, a story about real life" (Medawar, 1982, pp.110–111). Thus, the difference between astronomy and astrology is not as great as we first imagined; in both cases people are looking to the heavens and creating stories to explain what they see.

We now recognize even more the importance of nourishing children as tellers of scientific tales. We tried to encourage this storytelling stance in a variety of ways throughout the year: We invited children to interpret the intriguing history of the bluebirds; we encouraged them to create theories to explain current observations, such as the aggressive behavior of birds at the feeder or the rumpled feather of a finch; we invited children to explain the significance of the data they had collected about bluebirds. Children wove fiction and nonfiction together in interesting ways as they told their stories. For instance, after Lily discussed the findings of her bluebird data she wondered why the English sparrow and the bluebird were enemies and suggested that maybe they had an argument long ago. Eric and Shawn wrote "Last Action Swan," which incorporated a variety of facts about swans to tell an imaginative story. Hearing their tale and listening to E.B. White's *The Trumpet of the Swan* gave us all a better appreciation for the role of fact in nonfiction; we were also learning how much fiction there was in fact; theories are merely "fictions of limited truth" (Rosen, 1984, p. 17). At one time it was an accepted fact that the earth was the center of the universe, that the atom could not be split, and that the continents never moved. However, science changes and the stories must continually be revised. Children must be supported to be active storytellers by constructing their own theories and interpretations for explaining their world.

Science as a Living Tension

One other aspect concerning our changed view of science was the productive tension that we saw occurring between theory and observation. For instance, when we first saw the wing-waving of the bluebirds, we theorized that it represented the characteristic role of the male showing off for the female. As we read further we learned that the wing-waving was also a form of communication and we returned to the window with new eyes to see how this communication was demonstrated. On another occasion Tony theorized that the brown thrasher and the bluebird were enemies because he saw the latter frequently fly away when the thrasher entered the yard. However, later in the spring he changed his theory when he noticed the thrasher hopping around the bushes at the base of the blue-bird pole. He interpreted this behavior to mean that the thrasher was protecting the bluebirds from the threat of an attack by the starlings. Tony's new information about the predatory behavior of starlings caused him to change his theory and reinterpret the events that he saw transpiring.

This tension between theory and observation is a dynamic part of scientific inquiry and is nicely demonstrated today by the new measurements that astronomers are receiving from the Hubble Space Telescope. These measurements seem to indicate that the universe may be much younger than scientists had believed possible—only eight to twelve billion years old versus the previous estimate of fifteen to eighteen billion years (the date for the oldest known stars). If these measurements are correct, they may force scientists to revise their theories of how stars evolved and to reexamine the widely accepted model of creation, the Big Bang theory itself (Sawyer, 1994). Likewise, the children had constructed theories to explain their own observations. They kept returning to the window with new theories in mind, watching to confirm, revise, or abandon the theories they had proposed. This shuttling back and forth among observations, theories, and further observations is the dynamic tension that all scientists must live with and one that we must continue to cultivate in our classrooms.

A Renewed Appreciation for the Power of Models

Throughout the year the children constructed a variety of models about different aspects of birds. As we reflected on these models we realized that they served many purposes. When we hung Rhiannon's life-size models of various common birds from the ceiling the children often used them to identify a species or to support a description. Children would point to the model of the robin and remark, "The bird I saw was about as big as that robin." Danny referred to one bird he saw as "about the size of those two birds combined," referring to two of the models; later he described the stripes of another he observed as "kind of like the stripes of that bird there," again using the models as his reference point.

Sometimes the models served to confirm an hypothesis. When several children were trying to identify a mystery nest, Amanda used her models of goldfinch eggs to see if they would make an appropriate fit inside the nest. Our graph paper model of the forest fragmentation problem served to encourage a sense of playfulness with the attributes of this situation. Since scientific models do not replicate natural conditions completely, the children questioned the assumptions of the model and then tried cutting up the forest in different ways to see what effect that would have on the problem. Models can also serve to challenge previously held assumptions. For instance, Nikki had thought that all eggs were the same size until she sketched a variety of life-size drawings, and several of her classmates made models of these eggs from play dough.

Models also enabled learners to make personal comparisons with a particular measurement. When we stapled onto the ceiling the eight-foot wing span of the trumpeter swan, the children would often stand underneath it, look up, and stretch out their own arms for comparison. There is a fascination with comparing ourselves with other phenomena in the natural world and models invited this potential for constructing these personal benchmarks. Lastly, models encouraged the inclination to examine the extremes of a particular attribute. For instance, when the children made the life-size model of the eagle's nest they wanted to solve "the ultimate problem" of how many hummingbird eggs would fit inside a nest that large. Life-size models can prompt an interest in comparing the smallest and largest of a particular kind of animal. Often we do not know a species very well until we have the opportunity to compare it to other species. Models can serve to stir up this talk of comparing, estimating, and predicting. In the future we want to encourage children to construct models of other phenomena so that we can learn more about this potential for exploring scientific ideas.

Benefits of a Long-Term Study

Scientific inquiry takes time, and the experience with birds gave us a fresh appreciation for the benefits of long-term studies in school. Only over time can learners construct generalizations, revise thinking, and become proficient in using tools. It is more likely that these benefits will come to fruition with the support of a strong social community. Thus, we have come to believe that it is essential for schools to provide regular opportunities for extended studies. Of course, teachers face the tensions of addressing curricular mandates and managing time, so it is also important to investigate practical solutions to enacting long-term studies in the face of the realities of day-to-day constraints.

A Long-Term Study Provides Time for Learners to Construct Generalizations Rather than Simply to Accumulate Facts

Harrington (1994) labels this difference as the ability to reason. He likens facts to individual threads on a loom, but it is generalizations that weave the facts together. The fabric remains on the loom as learners continue to struggle with anomalies and draw new conclusions. The notion of time is implied in Harrington's metaphor; learners need time to add to the fabric on the loom. We saw this developing fabric again and again during the year as the children constructed and revised theories about what they observed and read.

A Long-Term Study Supports Learners in Exploring the Interconnectedness of the Natural World

Harrington writes, "Understanding means to know enough about something so that every part of it is seen in proper relationship to all the other parts and to the whole" (p. xi). Lily, for example, developed an appreciation for insects because of their relationship with birds. We adults shared this change in worldview. We were familiar with the facts in the children's science textbook, but as we followed the lives of birds, the facts took on new life. For example, in the chapter on animals, the text stated that there were 750,000 kinds of insects. It also mentioned that birds were important insect controllers. Without our study of birds, these facts might remain lifeless and unconnected in the book. We might not wonder, "*How* can there be so many insects in the world? *Why* are there so many insects in the world? Is there any relationship between the number of insects and the number of birds?" It was the study of birds that enabled us as adults to reason and to form generalizations. After the bluebird eggs hatched, we bought mealworms by the hundreds to set out on a tray for food. The class watched the adult bluebirds pick up nearly a dozen mealworms at a time to bring to the nestlings. We read in another resource book about bluebirds that each baby can consume 600-800 insects before it fledges. The data that we collected by watching our bluebirds and keeping records of the numbers of mealworms set out confirmed this fact. Suddenly we developed wondrous appreciation for the balance of nature. We could see with fresh eyes the relationship between the proportion of insects and birds among living creatures. This new world vision enabled us to be a different kind of teacher. We were sharing these facts out of wonder, and this wonder could only be nurtured by taking time to look closely, to read and reread, and to share in a collaborative community.

A Long-Term Study Creates Interdisciplinary Ties in a Natural Way

Rudy Mancke remarked, "One of the benefits of doing a long-term study is that the kids realize that this is not just a science project. This is all those other things too: math, and social organizations, populations, environmental stresses, and so on. We are all interpreters on the world." Rudy is stressing that the business of learning is interpretation. In that light, we can view the perspectives of different disciplines and the tools that characterize those disciplines as facilitators of our understanding. In trying to interpret the concept of forest fragmentation, it was helpful to construct mathematical models to investigate possible relationships. Students studied maps to draw conclusions about the ranges of different species. They constructed graphs and other visual displays to gain a perspective on the breeding cycle of bluebirds. The tools and strategies of various disciplines were helpful vehicles for the class to see new relationships. Only over time did these natural uses occur.

A Long-Term Study Supports Learners in Becoming Proficient with Resources

For instance, the field guides seemed to become a natural part of the children's identities as they used them over time. By the winter holidays many of the children owned their own field guides, which they kept in their desks. Other children depended upon guides and other resource books from the classroom library, but they, too, regularly kept a resource handy. Whenever a bird was mentioned during a discussion or during a read-aloud story, most of the children (almost in unison) flipped to a page that illustrated that particular species and held it up in the air. This "visual chorus" became a ritual over time. Whenever a guest speaker visited the class, they would remark to the adults afterwards that they were amazed at how quickly the children could locate the appropriate reference in such a wide variety of resources. We adults realized that the children's proficiency with resources only came because they had the opportunity to use these guides for numerous purposes over time. They browsed through the guides during silent reading time, and they used them to identify species that they saw in the yard or read about in a book. They returned to these resources to answer questions about the ranges of birds, about their migration, flock behavior, and breeding habits. Most of all, the children used these guides because they served a need born in wonder, and over time the guides became part of the children themselves. Proficiency with tools and resources looks much different in the light of a long-term study.

A Long-Term Study Builds Community

Although we have described this sense of community in Chapter 5, we feel that it is important to recognize its role here as well. A sense of community supports a long-term study just as much as a long-term study supports the building of a community. It is a mutually beneficial relationship that highlights increased understanding in an increasingly collaborative community. Children recognized the advantages of sharing observations and theories over time, knowing that multiple perspectives gave them more ways to view the world.

A Long-Term Study Fosters the Attitude that Learning Never Ends

The last day of the school year brought this understanding into sharp focus for us as teachers. On days when most classes were merely packing books and giving good-bye hugs, our class was raising questions. Chris brought a nest that he had found on the ground after a storm. He wanted his classmates to try to identify it. Eric sketched directions for building his own mealworm tray, and he asked to take part of the class's supply home so that he could feed the birds in his yard. We showed a video clip that we had recently shot for the children to interpret. The film showed a strange incident when one of the bluebird fledglings had caught his foot on the wire and flipped upside down. Both parents frantically wing-waved to each other, and the male pecked at the baby's feet until the bird fluttered off and then flew back to the wire. After the film, the children offered theories to explain how the parents coped with this dangerous situation. The clock ticked by, and it was time to go. Clutching their certificates of ornithology, the bus riders left. Billy and Chris stayed behind, and joined by their mothers, we chatted about summer plans. Billy's mother whispered in our ears the secret of Billy's upcoming birthday gift: a pair of binoculars. The school year was over, but nurtured by a community of learners, there was still time to grow.

If long-term studies are so important, then, how do we as teachers plan for them? What about district curricular mandates and the constraints of time? Perhaps if we had tried to preplan the "year of the birds," we may not have dared to embark upon this journey. As interest in birds mounted, we found ways to accommodate the busy schedule of school, and by doing so, we learned some practical applications of enacting long-term investigations. We already believed in offering choice during Writers' Workshop, so observing birds during that time was quite feasible. Most classrooms provide time for class meetings and sharing of personal events. In our class that time became an opportunity to share observations and questions about birds from home. The district mandates United States geography in the fourth grade. Birds became a lens to compare and contrast the various regions of our country. Children were also required to study perimeter, area, statistics, and ratio. Through a study of the birds, we were able to use mathematical concepts and strategies as tools to draw conclusions and make connections. However, we never felt compelled to force a connection; we had time as teachers to wait for a fitting opportunity to highlight these ideas. It was comforting not to be rushed with a study of birds in order to "finish the unit on time." The study followed a natural ebb and flow of interest. There were times when we did not see many birds or when the class focused on other issues. The children always knew, however, that the topic of birds was part of our group identity, even if it was not always at the forefront of our current attention. An interesting observation, or someone's new book, would refocus our attention, and the class would be off on another related adventure.

A Final Reflection: Revisioning a Sense of Wonder

Throughout this book we have paralleled the experiences of children with stories from the field of science in order to legitimize the scientific thinking of these young learners. However, we found that the most significant parallel was a sense of wonder; it was the most basic and most essential tie that bound the children and the scientific community together. Just as children show sophisticated thinking in the act of theory building, so too professional scientists reveal a childlike wonder in viewing the stars. We have come to appreciate the adult in the child and the child in the adult. A sense of wonder and an inquiring mind make us all full-fledged members of the scientific community.

Our year with the birds convinced us that a sense of wonder was the bedrock of an inquiring mind. Wonder is the force that not only sets inquiry in motion but also nourishes its growth. For this reason we placed wonder at the center of our model of a flower (see Preface). It grows out from the center as the instigating force but also holds the seed for continued growth. When we heard the sounds of birds in a flock, touched the soft lining of a nest, or saw the speed of a humming-bird's wings, we did so in wonder. It was a feeling about the world that permeated the scientific lives we were living out in this classroom community. Without the cultivation of this sense of wonder and awe about the natural world there is no changed view of the world. There may be fun activities, hands-on materials, and informative field trips, but without the wonder the knowledge that we gain has a hollow and empty ring to it.

Rudy Mancke learned early in life that it was this fascination for the mysteries of the world that nourished him as a learner. When he came home one day with a big stack of books from the local library his mother said to him:

> "You know, Rudy, I'm getting a little worried about you. I'm worried that you're doing so much learning that maybe the mystery will be gone out of the world and it won't be the wonderful world without the mystery."
>
> As Rudy reflected on this advice he remarked, "Mom was right on most things, but you know something, when you start reading and learning, the world is more mysterious than it's ever been. There are greater mysteries there than I had first supposed . . . There's no way that we'll ever clear up all of those mysteries, and I love them. I was reading a book in which the author was say-ing that knowledge was like a little island. You keep building on to this island of knowledge. But this island is in a massive, dark, rolling ocean of mystery . . . When you add to your island of knowledge you simply touch more of the ocean of mystery. The world gets more mysterious, not less mysterious."

It was this sense of wonder, awe, and mystery about the world that makes learners want to ask questions about what they are observing. A sense of wonder keeps pushing us to inquire further. Thus, we do not inquire to know, but we know in order to inquire.

Like Rudy, the more the children noticed the more questions they raised: Why do the chickadees take a seed and fly away while other birds stay and eat? Why do juncos fly in a flock? Why do cardinals always seem to come in pairs? It is this inquisitive attitude that characterizes how scientists take in the world:

> The naturalist biologist walks through a city park, across a suburban lawn, past an open shopping mall, and is half-consciously wondering: Why two leaves instead of three? Why pink flowers instead of white? Why does the plant turn this way instead of that way? Such rumination goes on without end in the scientist's mind, a continuous accompaniment to the rhythm of daily life. Whatever a scientist is doing—reading, cooking, talking, playing—science thoughts are always there at the edge of the mind. They are the way the world is taken in; all that is seen is filtered through an ever-present scientific musing. (Gornick, 1983, p. 15)

Learners raise these kind of questions naturally when they are given the opportunity to look closely at the world. It is this continual paying attention and asking questions about how the world works that drives learners forward in wanting to know more.

Rett described a theory as "a wonder based on what you know." His comment captures again the central role of wonder in a scientist's life. Theories are not cold, detached descriptions of the world but rather the natural consequences of a wondering mind. It is this sense of wonder that comes first. Gary Zukav confirms this notion when he shares what physicists really do:

> These people are engaged in extremely interesting adventures that are not that difficult to understand. True, *how* they do what they do sometimes entails a technical explanation which, if you are not an expert, can produce an involuntary deep sleep. *What* physicists do, however, is actually quite simple. They wonder what the universe is really made of, how it works, what we are doing in it, and where it is going, if it is going any place at all. In short, they do the same things we do on starry nights when we look up at the vastness of the universe and feel overwhelmed by it and a part of it at the same time. That is what physicists really do, and the clever rascals get paid for doing it. (Zukav, 1979, p. 3)

The wellspring of inquiry is not facts, theories, or scientific principles but a sense of wonder. It might involve wondering how a bird can crack open a seed without a set of hands to accomplish the task, or how long it would take to travel to the nearest star, or how a spider is able to build an intricate web, or how a honeybee can construct hexagonal cells. Einstein speaks of this sense of wonder that he felt as a young child:

> A wonder of such nature I experienced as a child of four or five years when my father showed me a compass. That this needle behaved in such a determined way did not at all fit into the nature of events . . . I can still remember—or at least I believe I can remember—that this experience made a deep and lasting impression upon me. Something deeply hidden had to be behind things . . . (Arendt, 1977, p. 4)

As we began to look closely at the world, ask questions and consult resources to answer our questions, we found that the new information we uncovered did not detract from the wonder, as Rudy's mother had feared, but instead increased the wondrous halo that surrounded the event in the first place. For instance, as they looked out the window the children were amazed at the speed of the hummingbird's wings; when we read that the wings beat eighty times per second we returned to the window with an even greater sense of awe for these marvelous birds.

Even facts are wondrous things. Thomas Locker, a well-know illustrator of children's books, addresses this point. He recently collaborated with a science teacher to create a book about trees, and he states in the Author's Note, "I was amazed to discover that the more scientific facts I learned, the deeper my sense of wonder became" (Locker, 1995). Richard Feynman speaks of a similar feeling when he describes the aesthetic perspective of a scientist. He has a friend who is an artist. This person questions that Feynman doesn't really have a sense of what is beautiful in the world, such as a flower, because scientists are always analyzing too much. Feynman disagrees:

> First of all, the beauty that he sees is available to other people—and to me, too, I believe. Although I might not be as refined aesthetically as he is, I can appreciate the beauty of a flower. But at the same time, I see much more in the flower than he sees. I can imagine the cells inside, which also have a beauty. There's beauty not just at the dimension of one centimeter; there's also beauty at a smaller dimension. (1988, p. 11)

Feynman is fascinated with the action of the cells; he marvels at how the colors of flowers have evolved to attract insects. His knowledge of science served to increase his "excitement and mystery and awe of a flower" (1988, p. 11). The wonder and awe that we express comes about because we have taken the time to pay attention to a part of the world that we found intriguing. A natural outcome of this focused attention is that we come to appreciate and value birds, flowers, or plants in a new, more empathetic way. Shunta eloquently addressed this point when she was trying to describe the wing-waving behavior of bluebirds to another teacher at the school: "They don't speak with their beaks, but they use their wings to talk with each other, 'cause I've seen them, whenever the male waves his wing to talk to somebody, he just lifts up his wing, and that's called wing-waving. If the female sees him, she waves back. They wing-wave back. That's why I think they are talking to each other, 'cause it really looks like it. *You have to see it to know it.*" Shunta's description shows how she is cultivating "the art of becoming personally aware" (Harrington, 1994, p. 142) of her surroundings in an aesthetic, emotional way. This intimate feeling for birds and their unique behavior is parallel to the feeling that Barbara McClintock has for plants:

> No two plants are exactly alike. They're all different, and as a consequence, you have to know that difference. I start with the seedling, and I don't want to leave it. I don't feel I really know the story if I don't watch the plant all the way along. So I know every plant in the field. I know them intimately, and I find it a great pleasure to know them . . .
> Animals can walk around but plants have to stay still to do the same things, with ingenious mechanisms . . . Plants are extraordinary. For instance,

. . . if you pinch a leaf of a plant you set off electric impulses. You can't touch a plant without setting off an electric impulse . . . There's no question that plants have [all] kinds of sensitivities. They do a lot of responding to the environment. They can do almost anything you can think of. (Freeman & Keller, 1995, pp. 199–200)

Another important aspect of wonder is a deep respect and appreciation for the beauty of the world. Rhiannon demonstrated this dimension of wonder one morning in February when she was lining up to attend music class. As she stood in line she kept looking out the window at the male bluebird that was perching on the roof. He faced east as he usually did, his rusty red breast glowing radiantly in the fresh light of a new day. Rhiannon took one more glance as she passed the window and then turned to David and said in her soft voice, "The bluebird is one of the most beautiful things I've ever seen in the world." She paused for a second and then qualified her response, "The bluebird *and* the hummingbird, I mean." Learners must come to see that the beauty of the world lies all around them. As the maxim says, "Diving and finding no pearls in the sea, Blame not the ocean, The fault lies with thee." What a shame it is to live a life and never really see it. Leo Buscaglia used to say that his father asked family members to tell about something they had seen that day that they had never seen before. This was a requirement at the dinner table each night. Likewise, in an inquiry classroom there is the expectation that learners will see new things, create fresh wonders, and uncover unappreciated mysteries each day. This expectation is reminiscent of a game that Annie Dillard played when she was a little girl. She used to hide a penny in the hollow of a tree or a crack in the sidewalk; she would then take a piece of chalk and draw huge arrows on the sidewalk in hopes that the first lucky passer-by would receive this "free gift from the universe" (Dillard, 1974, p. 15). Later on in her life she realized that her game was really a metaphor for noticing and celebrating the beauty of this world:

> It is still the first week in January, and I've got great plans. I've been thinking about seeing. There are lots of things to see, unwrapped gifts and free surprises. The world is fairly studded and strewn with pennies cast broadside from a generous hand. But—and this is the point—who gets excited by a mere penny? If you follow one arrow, if you crouch motionless on a bank to watch a tremulous ripple thrill on the water and are rewarded by the sight of a muskrat kit paddling from its den, will you count that sight a chip of copper only, and go your rueful way? It is dire poverty indeed when a man is so malnourished and fatigued that he won't stoop to pick up a penny. But if you cultivate a healthy poverty and simplicity, so that finding a penny will literally make your day, then, since the world is in fact planted with pennies, you have with your poverty bought a lifetime of days. It is that simple. What you see is what you get. (Dillard, 1974, p. 16)

The expectation that we will find new and beautiful things together is an important attitude in a classroom of inquiring voices. Together we will find new treasures every time we turn over the next rock or look out the window one more time. If we expect the unexpected we will keep finding new splendors at every turn.

And so we have come to see wonder as a many-faceted thing: a persistent attitude of questioning, a fascination for how things work, an appreciation for beauty and an attraction to the mysteries that surround us all. Wonder was the way we took in the world, and it bound us together as a community. For instance, Mr. Kelly, owner of the local bird store, once told us that talking to one of our students, Rett, was "just like talking to an adult." We reflected upon his comment and tried to understand what it was that allowed two people, separated by a span of over fifty years, to converse as equals? We realized it was their common urge to follow their curiosity, pose their own questions, and venture their own hypotheses; together they raised the unanswerable questions, admired the unfathomable beauty, and shared the inexplicable wonder. These are the ties that brought us together as fellow learners and compassionate human beings. Wonder was the unchanging center that cut across all that we said and did. It was unchanging, not in the sense that it was not dynamic, and fluid, but unchanging in the sense that it was always there, a permanent and essential part of how we viewed the world. It was through wonder that we learned that the real sustaining force of inquiry lies at the window because that is where learners meet the world face-to-face.

Epilogue:
Another Year Begins

On several occasions we shared highlights of this school year with Carolyn Burke of Indiana University. Even though she recognized many benefits in what we were describing, she reminded us at the end of one of our conversations, "You know, you can't do birds again next year." We have always appreciated Carolyn's perspective because she has a knack for nourishing people's growth. This comment was no exception. She did not want us to become too comfortable with the topic of birds. Rather, she wanted us to reflect more deeply about the process; birds acted as a placeholder for inquiry but they were not inquiry itself. To prevent this experience from being reduced to just a unit on birds we needed to reflect on the nature of this yearlong study and draw out of it the key conditions for supporting an inquiry stance. And that is what this book has been about. The chapters serve to emphasize these important conditions. However, the following year we were still left with the challenge of how to transform these ideas about inquiry into a new context. It was a productive tension that we looked forward to with some excitement as well as some apprehension. How do we carry the spirit of inquiry learning into a new setting with different children who have different experiences and interests (as well as into a new classroom setting, since Phyllis was moved from the portable to a classroom within the main building)?

Following a New Direction

We did not abandon birds completely. We still wanted to have the observation of birds as one invitation for the children. Phyllis had one large window in her room that faced some woods on the back side of the school. We placed two stick-on bird feeders on this window and we soon attracted a variety of species. We also found

137

that the wooded environment (versus the more open sanctuary of the previous year) gave us the opportunity to observe a variety of woodpeckers, including the yellow-bellied sapsucker, which feasted on the fruit of the persimmon tree. The children compared the size, coloring, and eating habits of all the woodpeckers that we spotted. This new venue for viewing birds also gave the children a unique opportunity to track their flight pattern as different species approached and left the feeder. Several students noted these patterns in the class journal, documenting the location, direction, pattern, and duration of these flights.

Another new dimension of this bird-watching was the proximity of the birds; the window feeders enabled us to see the birds close-up. This unique vantage point opened up new explorations to pursue. For instance, the children were intrigued with why some birds preferred one seed over another; they examined the remains of the birdseed trays each morning and saw that the sunflower seeds were more popular than the safflower seeds. However, they had observed that some species, such as the tufted titmouse, seemed to prefer the safflower. Their observations led them to wonder what kind of ratio of sunflower/safflower seeds was the best to use in our trays. As a result, they gathered data on seed preferences, analyzed the contents of the seed trays, and developed their own best ratio to meet the needs of these species in this particular locale.

Even though birds were an ongoing fascination throughout the year, there was another topic that really captured the interests of these students. And yet, ironically, it was the birds that proved to be the catalyst for this new scientific adventure. It happened about the first week of school. Jon was sharing his description of a hummingbird that he saw at the feeder and he wrote that "Its back was green like emeralds." Two days later Colby brought to school his gem collection so he could show the class what emeralds really looked like (of course, his polished stones were not really emeralds but they did have a similar color). The children were fascinated with his rocks and several students offered to share their collections as well. During the next month different children kept bringing in rocks from home. They loved describing the features of each rock and telling why certain ones were their favorites. We soon realized that our focused study of the year ought to be rocks (and we smiled to each other that we stumbled upon this topic through a discussion about birds)!

We learned that the school had a collection of rocks and minerals, which we brought to class for the children to observe. Their written descriptions revealed a number of interesting features about these rocks. The children noted the color in different ways: Jon: "It has white scratches on it;" Ryan: "My rock is burgundy red and shiny;" Selita: "It has gray and white mixed up together;" Justin: "My rock is black and white and a touch of red and there is a splash of brown . . . At the top it is mixed with white and brown and just a drop of black. There is equal lines of white but there is not a equal line of black." Of course, many of the words they used in their descriptions, such as *splash* and *burgundy*, are metaphorical. As we read the rest of their journal entries we found other metaphors: Jesse: "It looks like it has rivers and streams on the side;" Catherine: "My rock is shaped like a place in the mountains called Sliding Glass Rock;" A.J.: "Mine is as long as a humming-bird." As in the study of the birds we saw again the natural use of metaphor by children when they are invited to describe phenomena in their own way. We were also struck by the children's ability to describe the various colors of the rocks. In order to extend this interest we bought colored pencils that covered a range of grays, browns, and oranges. These new tools enabled them to be more precise with their drawings. Here again we witnessed the functional use of tools as the children strived to make their descriptions more accurate.

After children observed closely we invited them to record a wonder they had about rocks. Some of these questions included:

1. How old are rocks?

2. How are rocks made? I wonder how rocks are formed, and how they get big and small.

3. Where do rocks come from?

4. How can you tell if a rock came from a volcano?

5. How do rocks get crystals?

6. I was wondering how rocks get their colors?

7. How can we tell if Native Americans used this rock?

8. How do rocks get cracks?

9. Why do rocks break in different ways?

10. I wonder how rocks are part of earthquakes?

These queries were quite diverse and provided several avenues to explore. Again it was the children's observations and wonders that set the direction for us to follow.

The attributes of color, size, content, condition, and age of rocks led us inevitably to investigate weathering, erosion, and the rock cycle. These concepts were all a natural part of the larger geological tale; the children wanted to know more because these ideas were serving to fill in some of the missing parts of the story. One of the results of the bird study was that children could look at birds in their own yard and start to tell stories about what they saw, relating it to some of the issues we discussed in class, such as predation, territoriality, feeding, communication, male/female roles, and so on. We wanted to nourish this same storytelling disposition in geology as well. Our goal was for children to be able to look at a rock, a mountain, or a cut along a roadside, and construct a plausible story about it. In short, we wanted them to be readers of the world. Our study with the birds helped us better understand this important idea.

Crystals were of particular interest to the children. Several students shared different kinds of crystals with the class, and we all marveled at their shape, size, and luster. To extend this interest further we cracked a calcite crystal to show its unique lines of cleavage. We had witnessed this breaking of calcite on a film that we saw and wanted to try the experiment ourselves. After we struck the crystal with a hammer and opened the towel that surrounded it, the children gasped at the results (even though they knew what to expect from the video). The crystal did not shatter but had broken into smaller pieces along parallel lines of cleavage. We broke some of these smaller pieces and discovered that they broke in the same manner. We invited the children to offer theories for why the calcite broke in this predetermined manner. Jon wrote that the "breaks were like a fault in an earthquake;" Catherine suggested that "maybe there is a special mineral in it;" Colby and others thought the shape of the crystal caused it to break in this way, but Jesse wrote, "I think this happens because rocks join together and heat and pressure make it a bigger rock." Cruz offered a theory that hinted at the molecular structure: "My theory is that it was formed that (way)." Ryan generalized the process by hypothesizing that "most minerals break (in this way) but stay the same shape. It reminds me of mica because when you break it, it stays the same shape." We knew from our study of the birds that providing time for the construction of theories was a crucial dimension of scientific communities. This conversation about the property of calcite raised some important questions for us to pursue: Are crystals programmed to break in predetermined ways? How are crystals able to grow in these particular ways? Do all crystals break in this kind of predictable way? Do crystals have lines in them that are similar to the fault lines in the earth? In what ways do heat and pressure affect the properties of rocks? Again, we did not know the answers to all these questions, but we were willing to find out because the children had raised them and wanted to know more. Again we remembered from the bird investigation that open-ended discussions such as these are generative enterprises and set the direction for further explorations.

Just as models were an important tool for us in understanding the birds, so too they were a valuable tool in learning about geology. After cracking this calcite we had the children make three-dimensional paper models of that calcite crystal. When Joel and Ryan put their models side by side, they were able to demonstrate the reverse process of breaking apart a calcite crystal. Excited about their connection they recruited the efforts of other class members and began to place more and more of the small models together to make a huge model of the crystal. Since the shape was a rhomboid with its characteristic sloping sides it took a lot of flipping and turning before the pieces fit together as they should. Alice saw that the model had "the same angles" as the real crystal, noting one of the key features of similar shapes. Catherine realized that if these models were placed together in another way "you could make thicker sizes" of the calcite crystal. Thus, the model helped her imagine other possible sizes for the crystal. The children knew that the faces of the crystal were similar to the shape of the parallelogram, one of the pattern block pieces they had used earlier in the year. However, Ryan tried to explain how this three-dimensional model was different from the flatter pattern block piece: "It's pointed out on the outside lines (the edges) . . . there are edges everywhere on this thing . . . the edges are all pointed out." The model provided the additional dimension of depth for the children to consider and again we noted the importance of having children explain this new attribute in their own language. Just like in our study of the birds we noted that three-dimensional models provide a unique perspective on the process. We also saw how mathematics was a natural part of our discussion because it helped us describe a crystal system that we all found wonderfully exciting.

Just as the children used mathematics to frame their understanding of geology, so too they used their knowledge of geology to help them describe some of their mathematical investigations. For instance, Sara used a geological analogy to explain a problem in geometry. She had been using pattern block pieces to make larger similar shapes. She found she could make larger squares with squares, larger triangles with triangles, and larger parallelograms with parallelograms. However, she could not make hexagons fit together to make larger and larger hexagons, and she explained the problem in this way: "It's kind of like breaking a rock because some rocks break into the same (shape) as the first one and some don't." Whitney noticed that if she placed four squares together she could "make a salt rock," remembering the cubes of salt that she had observed with a hand lens. When Catherine was building larger triangles out of smaller triangles she said that her successively larger patterns "looked like sedimentary rock." This study of rocks was beginning to confirm for us once again the important interdisciplinary ties that are possible in a long-term study.

The importance of not stepping in front of the struggle was demonstrated for us as the children continued to make careful observations of our rock collections. We invited the children to compare their rocks in different ways and then invent a way to display those comparisons. Maggie used a graph to show how much each rock sparkled; Gavin put his ear on his desk and tapped each rock lightly so he could listen for differences in sound. He found that one rock had a "deep sound," one had a "high sound," and the other had a "medium sound." Catherine was intrigued with this idea and used it on another occasion to show the differences in sound she heard in her set of rocks (Figure E-1). She developed a loudness scale and then described the sounds in metaphorical terms: "This rock sounds like

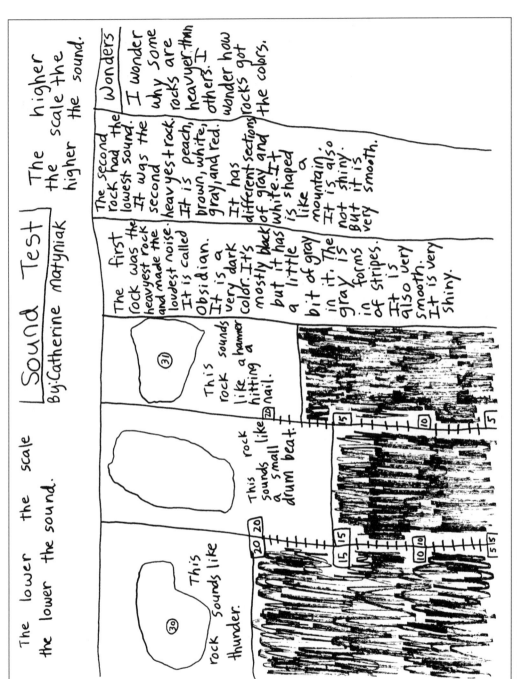

FIG E–1 *Catherine's Sound Test*

thunder. This rock sounds like a small drum beat. This rock sounds like a hammer hitting a nail." It was this initial interest in sound that caused David to wonder about the work of seismologists and their study of the earth's interior. Here again student and teacher were co-learners in this inquiry investigation.

Amy created another kind of scale to indicate differences in weight (Figure E-2). She explained that the lower the bar on the graph, the heavier the rock weighed because "when I put the rock in my hand, my hand went lower." She said that she always likes to see how much things weigh at her house; she often picks up bags of groceries to compare their weights. Although her method for displaying these weights seemed contradictory to us at first, her explanation made good sense. We were again thankful that we did not step in front of the struggle and be more directive in how children ought to classify their rocks and how they ought to visually represent those differences. Sara was interested in both these tests of sound and weight and combined them in a single representation (Figure E-3). She wrote that "A weighs less than B and C weighs less than all. Sound A was lower than B; C was less than A; B was higher than C." Her visual captures all the combinations that are possible in a succinct, clear manner. Sara was quite proud of her effort and wrote as part of her reflection, "I wonder if science people would think the same." By being involved in the process of scientific inquiry the children were again seeing themselves as legitimate members of the scientific community. In fact, the children created many other scales for rocks, such as roughness, sparkle, flatness, and color. Whitney used the feel of her rocks to develop a coldness test to show the "temperature" of each rock. Her test caused Phyllis to think about the conduction of heat with different substances, such as the cold feel of a metal chair or the warmer touch of a wooden desk. Later we learned that a test for jade is coolness. Student and teacher were forging new connections together, just as they did in their study of birds. Laura Jane tested how easily each rock scratched the paper and developed a line scale to indicate those differences. We were interested that the children not only developed tests for some of the standard attributes of rocks, such as luster, hardness, and color, but they also devised many others. They were learning more about the properties of rocks, as well as grappling with how to represent those attributes visually. As with our experiences with the bird study we learned the importance of having children live the life of scientists.

A Final Invitation to the Reader

We continue to try to build a classroom of inquiring voices. We continue to value wonder as the force that sets things in motion. We continue to look closely, ask why things are the way they are, and share our thinking in a collaborative community. We recognize inquiry not as a question or activity but as a perspective on

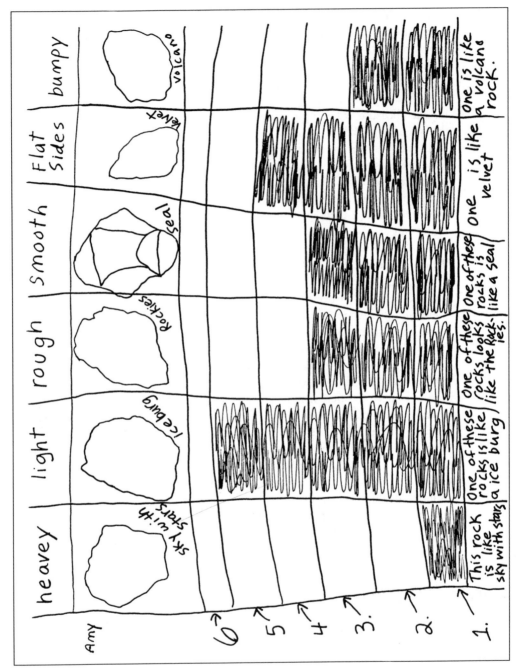

	heavey	light	rough	Smooth	Flat Sides	bumpy
Amy	sky with stars	iceburg	rockies	seal	velvet	volcano

1. This rock is like a sky with stars
2. One of these rocks is like a ice burg
3. One of these rocks is like the Rockies.
4. One of these rocks looks like a seal
5. One is like velvet
6. One is like a volcano rock.

FIG E–2   *Amy's Weight Test*

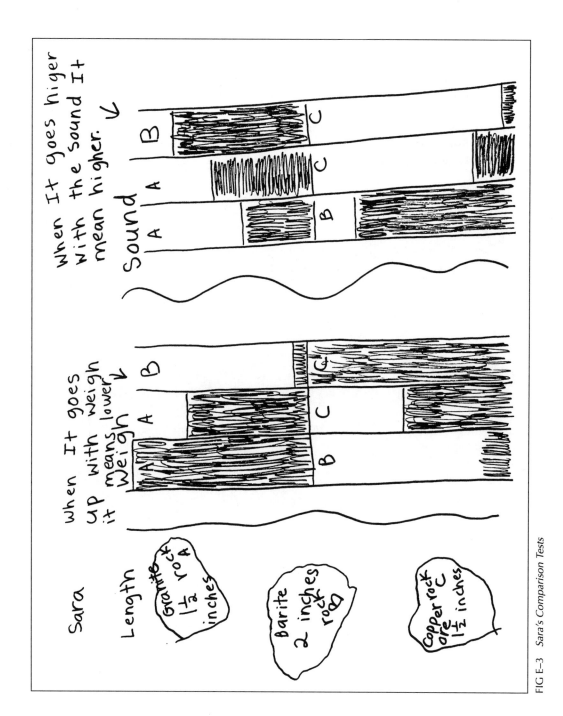

when It goes higer
with the sound It
mean higher. ↓

Sound

A   B   C
A   A   C
A   B   B   C

when It goes
up with weigh
it means lower ↓

Weigh

A   A   B
B   C   C

Sara

Length

Granite rock A
1½ inches

Barite 2 inches rock

Copper rock are C 1½ inches

FIG E–3   Sara's Comparison Tests

learning that celebrates surprise, thrives on doubt, and flourishes in tension. We have tried in this book to give you, the reader, a glimpse of inquiry learning without laying out a prescriptive formula to follow. If we have been successful, then we have left you with a tension of your own: how to operationalize a vision of learning into your own particular classroom. This is a productive tension that encourages us all to make connections and forge unforeseen possibilities. It is a tension that keeps us all young in heart and mind. It keeps us growing and learning. And it keeps us at the window.

Self-evaluation: Bird-Math Project (Measurement)

5-very much, or excellent   4-mostly, quite good   3-medium   2-could have done better   1-not much at all

1. I used my time well. I worked hard.   5   4   3   2   1

Comments _____

2. I worked well with others. I gave advice,   5   4   3   2   1
and I listened to others when needed.

Comments _____

3. I treated materials with respect.   5   4   3   2   1

Comments _____

4. I made my plans carefully.   5   4   3   2   1

5. On the back, write about ONE of the following. BE VERY SPECIFIC

In my bird-math project, I . . .
. . . figured out a problem
. . . learned a new strategy
. . . became better at measuring

APPENDIX B

Project Proposal Form

Field Research About Birds

My wonder is:

This wonder is interesting to me because:

My plan for investigating this wonder is (also indicate if you will do part at home):

My theory about this investigation right now is:

APPENDIX C

Bird Research Project

Requirements

You will show your findings about the questions and wonders that interested you on your Research Proposal in these ways:

1. Narrative (explanation of your findings in written form). You will *describe* what you have learned about your topic. Your report must be:
   —**In Your Own Voice.** Your report should sound like you talking and explaining your ideas to fourth graders.
   —**Written Clearly.** Your report must be written in a *logical order*, so that it is easy for an audience to understand. Your report should *give examples.* (For instance, if you are describing birds that glide as they fly, you should name birds that follow that pattern. If you are describing birds that come to the feeder in pairs, you should tell about times that you and class members have seen them come to the feeders in pairs.)
   —**Detailed, with information that is new to you and to the class.**
   —**Edited for spelling, capitalization, and punctuation (periods, question marks, commas, etc.)**
   —**Neat and pleasing to read.**

2. A *visual* that helps to show your information. The visual can be a model (such as Eric's model of flight patterns), a chart (for example, of favorite birdseed), a picture (of crested birds), a map (of where hummingbirds live and where they migrate), or diagrams (of feather parts, wing shape, etc.)

3. One or more "new wonders" or questions that now interest you because of your research. (Use a separate paper or at the end of your narrative. Shunta had a good example on her hummingbird report.)

4. A *list* of all resources that you used in your research.
Resources include:
Authors and titles of *books* and *videos*
Dates and locations of *observations*
Names of people interviewed

Some people will have more visual information; some people will have more written information. The important feature is that you have communicated the ideas that you learned from your research, and you show what you are now wondering.

_____

Signature of Parent

APPENDIX D

Bird Project Reflection

1. Describe what you are most pleased with about your project:

_____

_____

_____

2. I was most surprised when I learned _____

_____

3. I helped _____ by _____

_____

4. _____ helped me by _____

_____

5. When we shared our projects with the class, I learned _____

_____

6. If I did my project again, I would _____

_____

Forest Fragmentation Evaluation Rubric
Problem Solving, Perimeter, Area

Write your name and self-evaluate in the middle column. I will record my evaluation in the right-hand column. We will talk if our thinking is very different.

Category A: You made accurate calculations of your data.
Category B: You explained your discoveries in a systematic, clear way.
Category C: You made careful plans and used time wisely in following those plans.

5 – Excellent quality   3 – Satisfactory   1 – Inadequate

Category	Name	Dr. W.
A		
B		
C		

Parent Survey

Many times during the course of the year, the children related stories about birds from home. I am curious about your perspective on this yearlong adventure, and I would appreciate your thoughts on the following questions:

1. What have you noticed about your child at home during our study of birds?

2. How has your child involved you in the study of birds this year?

3. If you have other comments or a memorable story about your child and birds, please describe it here.

Student Survey

Reflecting on Our Yearlong Study of Birds

1. What do you notice now about birds that you didn't notice before this year?

2. Our class has spent many hours talking together about our wonders and theories. How did conversations about wonders and theories help you learn more about birds?

3. Different projects came up because of our study of birds. For example, we learned about forest fragmentation, sizes of eggs and nests, feathers, seed preferences, and patterns of nesting behavior, particularly of bluebirds. Describe how any of these projects helped you grow as a learner.

4. What did you do outside of class because of our study of birds?

5. Have you taught anyone else outside of class about birds? If so, who, where, what, and how?

6. What do you wonder now about birds?

7. What surprised or amazed you most in learning about birds?

8. What advice would you give next year's class if they wanted to learn about birds?

REFERENCES

ARENDT, H. 1977. *The life of the mind.* Vol. 1, *Thinking.* New York: Harcourt Brace Jovanovich.

ASSOCIATED PRESS. 1995. Scientist finds what may be the oldest fossil. *The State,* October 21: Columbia, SC.

ASSOCIATED PRESS. 1995. Brown dwarf discovered, but it may never be a star. *The State,* December 1: Columbia, SC.

BAYLOR, B. 1986. *I'm in charge of celebrations.* New York: Charles Scribner's Sons.

BEARDER, S. 1995. Calls of the wild. *Natural History. 104,* 48–56.

BEST, L. & HEIN, M. 1976. *Foundations of college chemistry.* Encino, CA: Dickenson Publishing Company, Inc.

BURKE, C. Conversation with authors, [10 April 1995].

CALKINS, L. 1994. *The art of teaching writing.* 2nd edition. Portsmouth, NH: Heinemann.

DEWEY, J. 1916/1966. *Democracy and education.* New York: The Free Press.

DHONDT, A. & LOWE, J. 1995. Variation in black-capped chickadee group size. *Birdscope. 9,* 7–8.

DiCHRISTINA, M. 1995. Unraveling the mystery of life. *Bostonia.* 14–18.

DILLARD, A. 1974. *Pilgrim at tinker creek.* New York: Bantam.

DONALDSON, M. 1978. *Children's minds.* New York: Norton.

EDGERTON, S. 1984. Galileo, Florentine 'desegno' and the 'strangspottednesse' of the moon. *Art Journal. 44,* 225–232.

EISNER, E. 1992. The misunderstood role of the arts in human development. *Phi Delta Kappan. 73,* 591–595.

FEYNMAN, R. 1988. *What do you care what other people think?* New York: Norton.

FLANDERS, M., The hummingbird, in Prelutsky, J. 1983. *The Random House book of poetry.* New York: Random House.

FREEMAN, W. & KELLER, E. 1995. *A feeling for the organism: The life and work of Barbara McClintock.* New York: W. H. Freeman.

GALLAS, K. 1995. *Talking their way into science.* New York: Teachers College Press.

GORMAN, C. & MAJOR, J. 1995. On its own two feet: Kenyan fossils suggest a new, earlier date when a human ancestor first walked upright. *Time, 146,* 58–60.

GORNICK, V. 1983. *Women in science: Portraits from a world in transition.* New York: Simon and Schuster.

GRAVES, D. 1989. *Investigate nonfiction.* Portsmouth, NH: Heinemann.

———. 1983. *Writing: Teachers and writers at work.* Portsmouth, NH: Heinemann.

GUIBERON, B. 1991. *Cactus hotel.* New York: Holt.

HARRINGTON, J. 1973/1994. *To see a world.* Spartanburg, SC: Holocene Publishing.

HARRISON, H. 1975. *Birds' nests.* Boston: Houghton Mifflin.

HAZEN, R. L. & TREFIL, J. 1991. *Science matters: Achieving scientific literacy.* New York: Doubleday.

HONG, L. 1993. *Two of everything.* Racine, WI: Albert Whitman.

HORNSTEIN, S. 1993. *Rocks tell stories.* Brookfield, CT: Millbrook Press.

JOHN-STEINER, VERA. 1985. *Notebooks of the mind.* New York: Harper and Row.

LOCKER, T. *Sky tree: Seeing science through art.* New York: HarperCollins.

MANCKE, R. Conversation with author, [20 February 1995].

McDONALD, K. 1993. Study of meteorite's crater renews debate on demise of dinosaurs. *The Chronicle of Higher Education, 40,* 6–7, 13.

MEDAWAR, P. 1982. *Pluto's republic.* Oxford: Oxford University Press.

MUIR, J. 1911. *My first summer in the Sierra.* Boston: Houghton Mifflin.

MURPHY, S. 1995. Closing address. Whole Language Umbrella Conference, Windsor, Ontario, July.

PETERSON, R. 1992. *Life in a crowded place.* Portsmouth, NH: Heinemann.

ROSEN, H. 1984. *Stories and meanings.* London: National Association for the Teaching of English.

ROSENBERG, K. & DHONDT, A. 1995. Seed preference: East versus west. *Birdscope. 9,* 1–3.

ROSENBERG, K., DHONDT, A., TESSAGLIA, D., LOWE, J., SENESAC, P., & GREGORY, S. 1995. A tale of four tanagers. *Birdscope. 9,* 4–5.

ROSENBLATT, L. 1978. *The reader, the text, the poem.* Carbondale, IL: Southern Illinois University Press.

SAWYER, K. 1994. Universe may not be so old after all. *The State,* October 27, Columbia, SC, A1, A10.

SMALLWOOD, W. & ALEXANDER, P. 1981. *Biology.* Morristown, NJ: Silver Burdett Company.

SMITH, F. 1988. *Joining the literacy club.* Portsmouth, NH: Heinemann.

The State. 1995. Erin fools forecasters. *The State,* August 2, Columbia, SC.

STOKES, D. & STOKES, L. 1991. *The complete guide to attracting bluebirds.* Boston: Little, Brown & Co.

TCHUDI, S., ed. 1993. *The astonishing curriculum: Integrating science and humanities through language.* Urbana, IL: National Council of Teachers of English.

TENNYSON, A., LORD. The eagle. In Daniel, M. 1989. *A child's treasury of animal verse.* New York: Dial.

TUFTE, E. 1983. *The visual display of quantitative information.* Cheshire, CT: Graphics Press.

WHITE, E.B. 1970. *The trumpet of the swan.* New York: Harper & Row.

WOODWARD, V. & SEREBRIN, W. 1989. Reading between the signs: The social semiotics of collaborative storyreading. *Linguistics in Education, 1,* 393–414.

YOLEN, J. 1990. *Birdwatch.* New York: Philomel.

ZUKAV, G. 1979. *The dancing Wu Li Masters.* New York: Bantam.